THE BEST OF
BUSTER

THE CLASSIC COMEDY SCENES DIRECT FROM THE FILMS OF
BUSTER KEATON

EDITED BY RICHARD J. ANOBILE

ELM TREE BOOKS
Hamish Hamilton/London

A DARIEN HOUSE BOOK

Design by Harry Chester Associates.

First published in Great Britain, 1976
by Elm Tree Books Ltd.
90 Great Russell Street
London WC1B 3 PT

ISBN 0 241 89519 7

Printed in the United States of America

All Buster Keaton films are available in 16 and 35mm (both sound—background
and musical effects—and silent versions) for theatrical, non-theatrical and
television viewing through:
    Mr. Raymond Rohauer
    Representative of Buster Keaton Productions, Inc.
    44 West 62nd Street, Suite 16B
    New York, New York 10023

INTRODUCTION
by
Richard J. Anobile

On October 4, 1895, during some undetermined hour in Piqua, Kansas, Joseph Francis Keaton poked his head into the world, a world which he was ultimately to suspect had been designed expressly for the purpose of keeping him involved in a never-ending chase. That chase was to take him in circles through the ages of mankind, at least filmically, and establish him as one of the cinema's most illustrious artists. That film existence would finally grind to a halt in 1966 somewhere around the seven hills of Rome.

But first young Joseph had to endure and survive the years on stage as a member of The Three Keatons, a vaudeville act in which he was partnered with his mother and father. Nightly and during matinees, Keaton would find himself flying through the air, and landing on his backside more times than not. All this was for the amusement of a music hall audience which gave no thought to, let alone comprehending, its part in shaping Keaton's outlook on life—that it was a series of chance happenings, some good, some bad, and others just inconvenient. And we should be mindful of our debt to the one and only Harry Houdini who, after witnessing the Keaton tyke's fall down a flight of stairs during a particularly arduous performance, nicknamed him "Buster."

Sometime during 1917 The Three Keatons found themselves at the end of their road. With bookings virtually nonexistent, Mom and Dad hightailed it home and Buster strolled off on his own. A chance meeting with Lou Anger in New York City (rumored to have been in the vicinity of 46th Street and Broadway), sealed his fate. Anger shuttled him off to 48th Street where an introduction to Fatty Arbuckle followed and Keaton's journey into cinematic immortality began. That afternoon Keaton appeared in his first film, Arbuckle's *The Butcher Boy.*

As it turned out, Buster Keaton rose to the apex of a very crowded profession which included such greats as Charlie Chaplin, Harry Langdon, Harold Lloyd and Laurel and Hardy. In my opinion, he towers over such names, especially because of his sensitivity towards humanity and the world it has created. He is not out to change anything. He wants only to exist.

Film by film, one hundred and twenty four of them, and without having complete control over the entire bunch, Keaton systematically follows through on his depiction of man against the world he has created for himself. A strong concept of human fallibility pervades every Keaton film: first he shows us ourselves through his character, then the system we have created. Keaton is so unrelenting in showing us ourselves that only laughter provides a respite, at least a temporary escape from sliding into terminal insanity.

In a Keaton film, laughter exists as part of a whole. It is not inserted merely to evoke a belly laugh or to bolster a sagging plot. Keaton's own films are brilliantly structured and the laughter he induces is always a natural extension of his characters and their actions. Keaton is not a comedian. He is a comic actor. There is a difference. His main concern is with telling a story, a humorous one, no doubt. But it is that story as a whole which is all important. Laughter at a Keaton film is laughter at the logical development of human folly.

Yet, for some years now, we have been paying homage to Charlie Chaplin and endowing him with all kinds, of attributes for which there is no uncontested evidence. Chaplin was a superlative performer and a fine comedian. He certainly was not a mindless performer. And possibly, he may have influenced Keaton. But it is Keaton who took performance and expertly blended it with film.

Keaton's innate awareness of structure produced scripts which are precise and unlarded. His sense of camera was astounding both on screen and as a director. And most unusual is that Keaton's ego seems almost subordinate. It is a tribute to the man that he was able to write, direct and act in many of his films without destroying either his performance or his directions, and without hogging every scene. Having a cerebral command of his medium, Keaton understood the importance of the other characters as individuals and as catalysts for his own screen character.

Simply, Keaton was a filmmaker. Chaplin is not. This then is the distinction between the two which sets them far apart in my mind. This is not to say that Chaplin's films were lacking imaginative ideas, but when it comes to direction and writing, Chaplin's hands are very heavy, indeed.

The main difficulty in bringing this book together was precisely the Keaton sense of structure in a film. Trying to find isolated scenes which would both capture the essence of Keaton and somehow stand on their own was difficult. So, while the publishers have chosen to title this book "The Best of Buster," I suggest that you think of it simply as "Some of The Best of Buster." To be sure, there are plenty of gags on which to pick up in a Keaton film. But they are part of a large fabric and extracting a few threads from such mass does not give an accurate impression of the whole pattern.

Therefore, I've concentrated on some lengthier scenes which I hope will give you a clue to what I see as Keaton's greatness. I hope that the following pages will spur you on down to your local retrospective house where, at some point — in large part due to the efforts of historian-collector Raymond Rohauer — Keaton films will surely play. In the meantime, turn these pages leisurely so as not to rush along what Keaton meant you to savor. He was a great believer in time and used it to full advantage to set a scene to carry forward a stream of thoughts which would all contribute to a gradual buildup of a humorous situation.

Time is the all-important element missing from much of today's film comedy. I speak of time in the sense of paced development, not the more common split-second "timing" favored today. The gag has become an end product. The story is secondary. The leisurely approach, missing in our society, is also missing in our films. Yet, that we can still laugh at Keaton's creations is proof positive that we have not lost our ability to allow an artist the time he needs to evoke our response. And it is further affirmation of Keaton's timeless appeal.

Not long ago I interviewed Gene Wilder. He had just completed directing his first film (*The Adventure of Sherlock Holmes' Smarter Brother*) from his own screenplay and in which he had the main role. After seeing a rough cut of some of the reels of his film I was impressed by the similarity of much of Wilder's work to that of Keaton. I mentioned this only to be told by Wilder that he had never seen a Keaton film. Of course, I urged him to do so. Yet, upon reflection, it occured to me that it was just as well that he hadn't seen a Keaton film. For then, Wilder might have been too self-conscious. Instead he followed his own inner feelings about structure precisely as Keaton had done.

Gene Wilder thus becomes the only American filmmaker currently carrying on the Keaton tradition. And although, in the end, his film displayed a heavy influence from the Mel Brooks slam bang school of comedy (logical, since Wilder had worked closely with Brooks) it nevertheless signaled the return to romanticism which has lately been nonexistent on the screen. Hopefully, as Wilder continues writing and directing he will grow more secure with his own style and allow himself the freedom of being his own man following his own instincts.

So here is what I hope will be a tribute to Buster Keaton. For some reason the image of him which remains fixed in my mind is that of Buster, now an old man, continually running over the seven hills of Rome in Richard Lester's 1966 film *A Funny Thing Happened on the Way to the Forum*. Here was Buster trudging alone with his wide eyes looking forever forward to a time when humanity would stop bedeviling itself. The chase goes on.

—Richard J. Anobile
Hollywood, California
June, 1976

ACKNOWLEDGMENTS

I wish to thank all those who have helped me realize this book.

The rights to produce this volume were granted by Raymond Rohauer; his cooperation in securing the necessary materials helped me meet my deadlines.

The negative materials were produced with care and precision by B&O Film Laboratories in New York under the supervision of Tony Bezich.

Once again Saul Jaffe and his Vitaprint Corporation performed marvelously in producing the frame blowups which are the essential factor is most of my book projects. Alyne Model worked at odd hours (by any definition), meticulously transferring my frame selections to the negative materials.

With characteristic elan and understanding, Harry Chester & Associates have designed a book which will enable the reader to follow the action in as natural a way as possible in this format. I am especially indebted to Alexander Soma of their staff.

Helen Garfinkle has coordinated a number of my projects; her friendship, wit and perspicacity have enhanced my work immeasurably.

—Richard J. Anobile

THE BEST OF
BUSTER

P. ÉTAIX

Joseph M. Schenck *Presents*

"Buster" Keaton

in

THE GOAT

RELEASED EXCLUSIVELY THROUGH

METRO PICTURES CORPORATION

COPYRIGHT BY
METRO PICTURES CORPORATION

Along Millionaires' Row

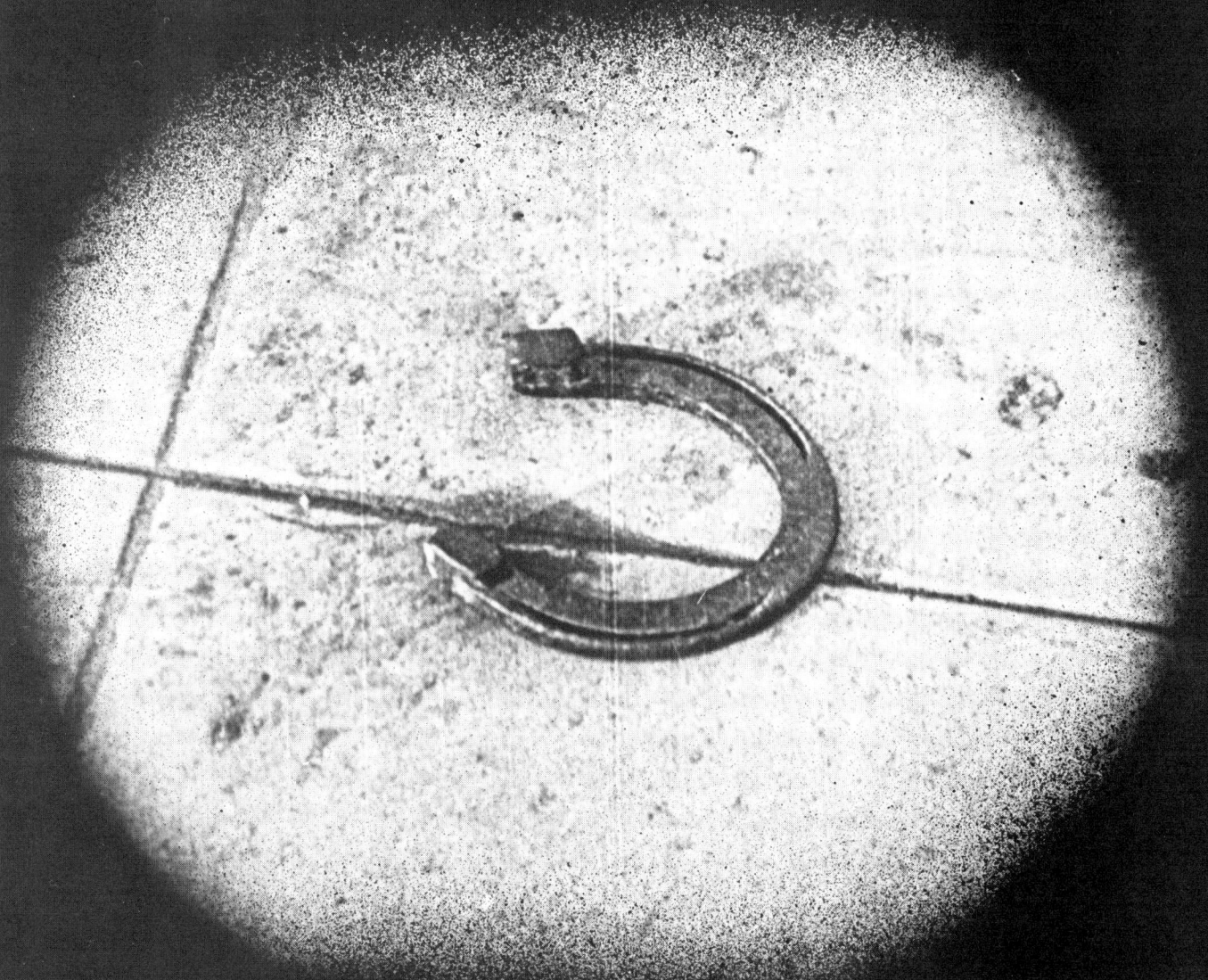

JOSEPH M. SCHENCK

presents

Buster Keaton

in

'Sherlock Jr.'

A Metro Attraction

*At the films outset
Keaton had been unjustly
accused of stealing his
girlfriend's father's
pocketwatch in order to
hock it to buy the girl
candy.*

*Now in the last reel, the
thief has been
discovered and the
girlfriend visits
Keaton in his projection
booth hoping to apologize
to him. Of course,
Keaton is happy to see
her and overcomes his
insecurity by taking his
cue from the leading man
on the screen; life
imitates art!*

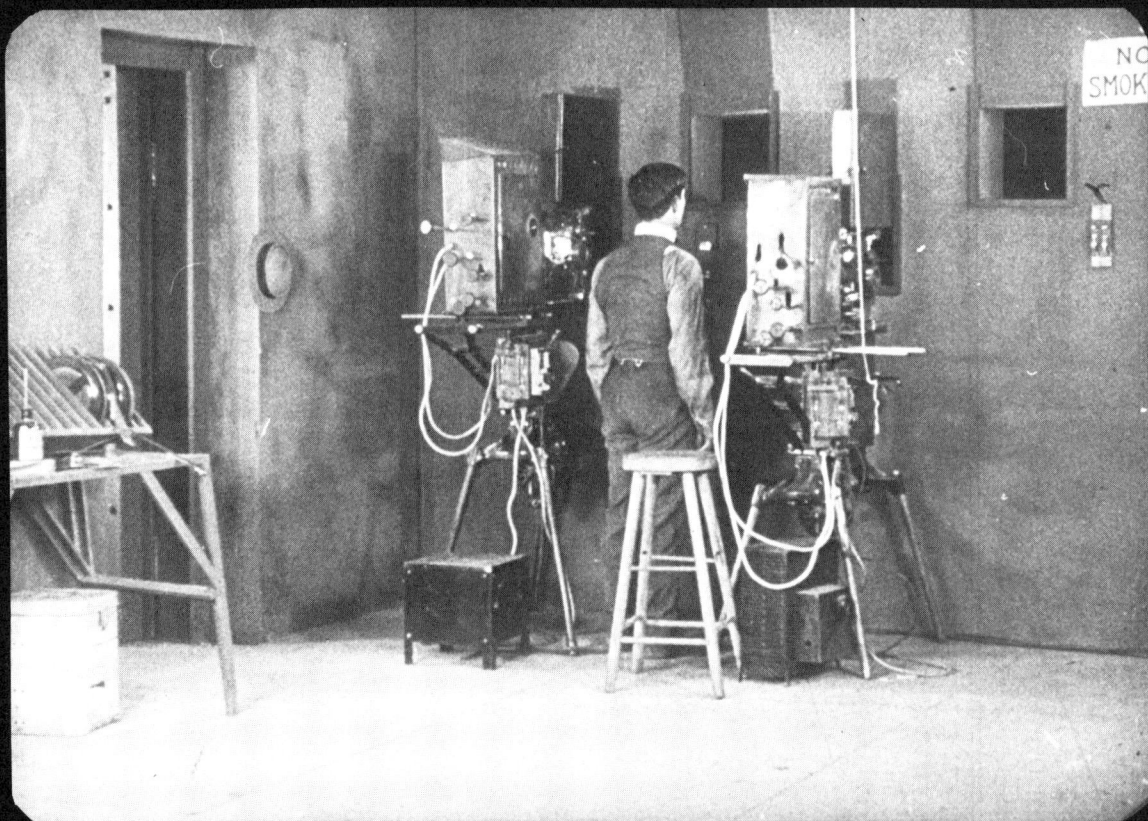

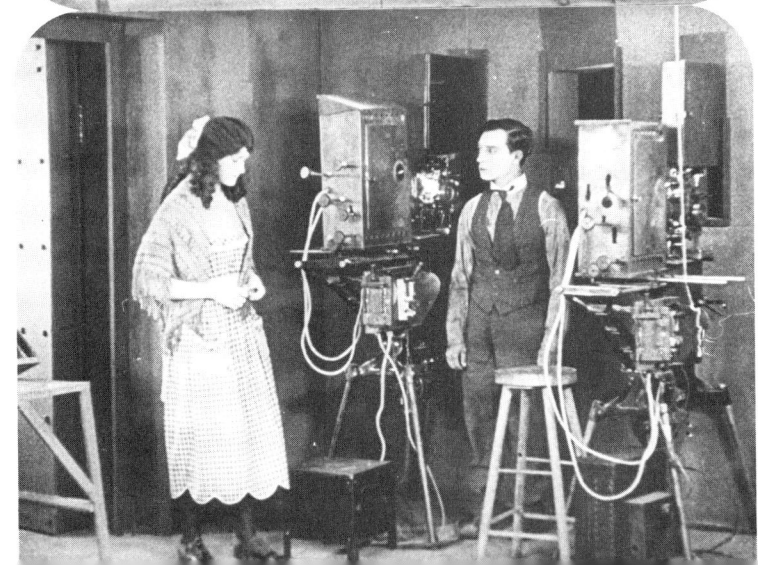

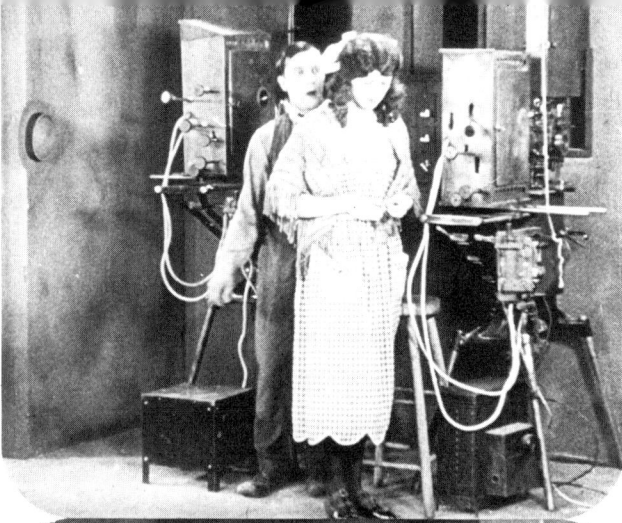

"Father sent me to tell you that we've made a terrible mistake——"

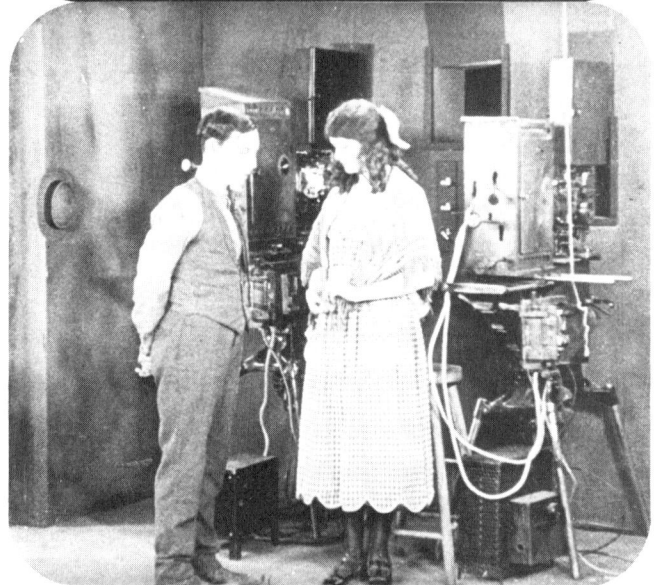

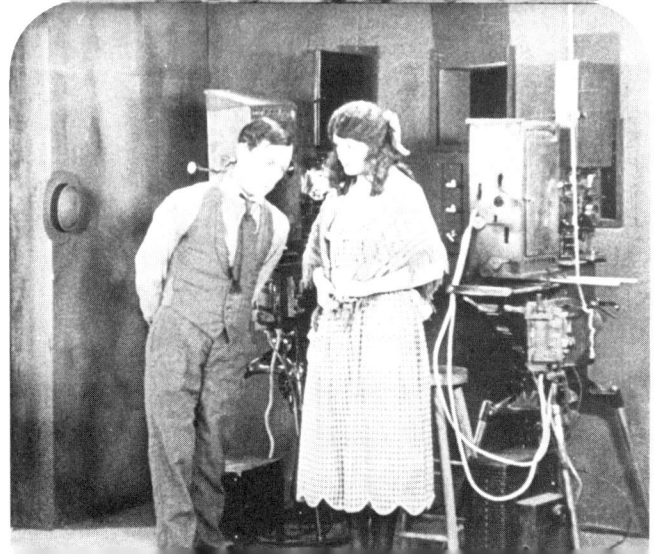

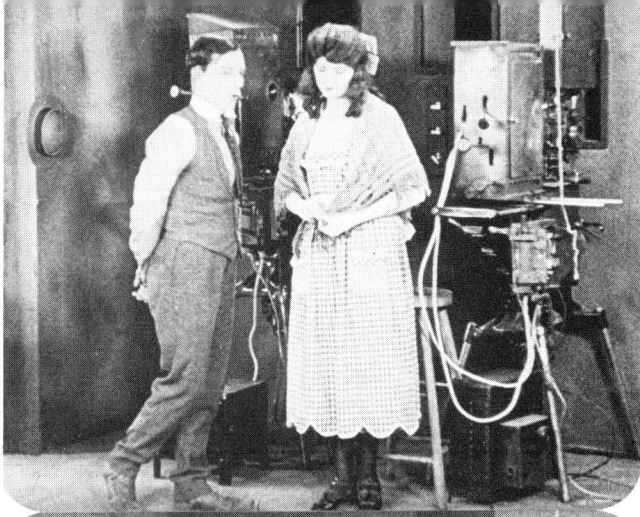

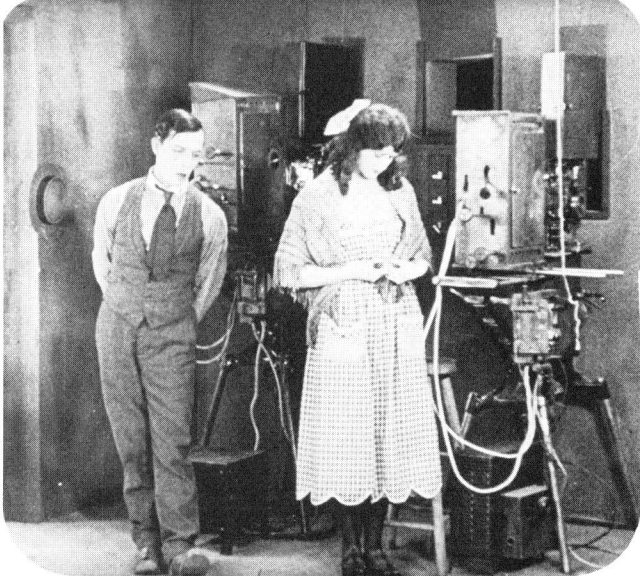

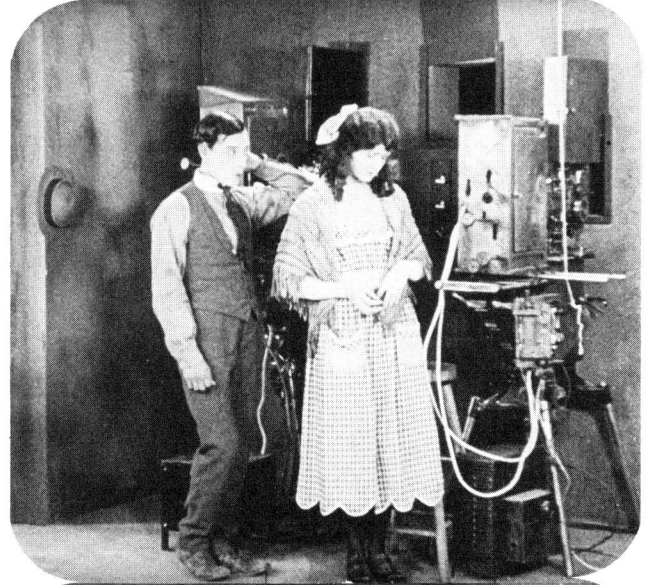

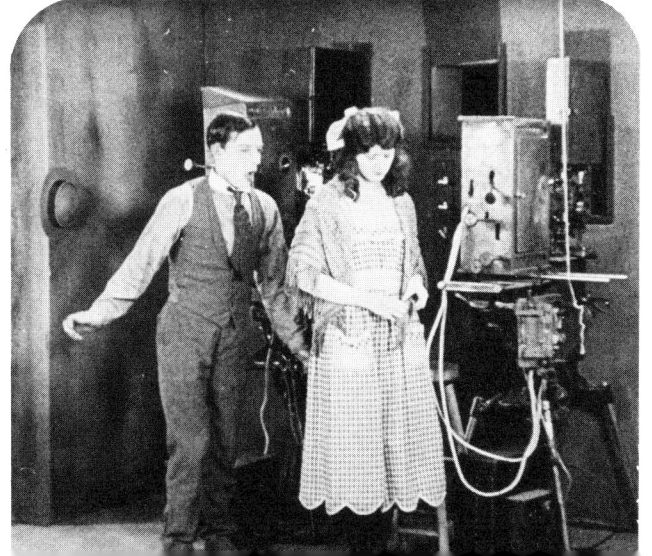

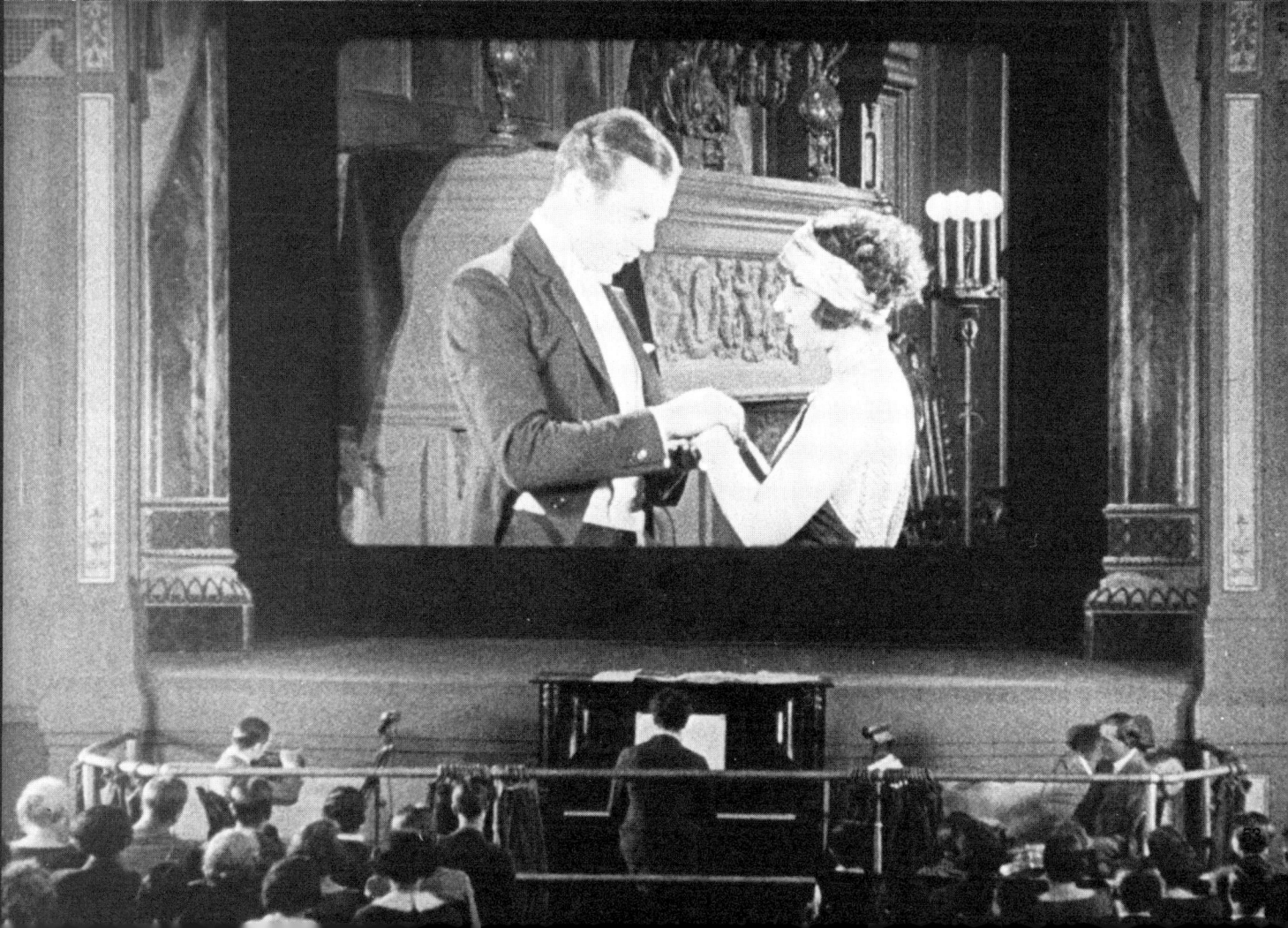

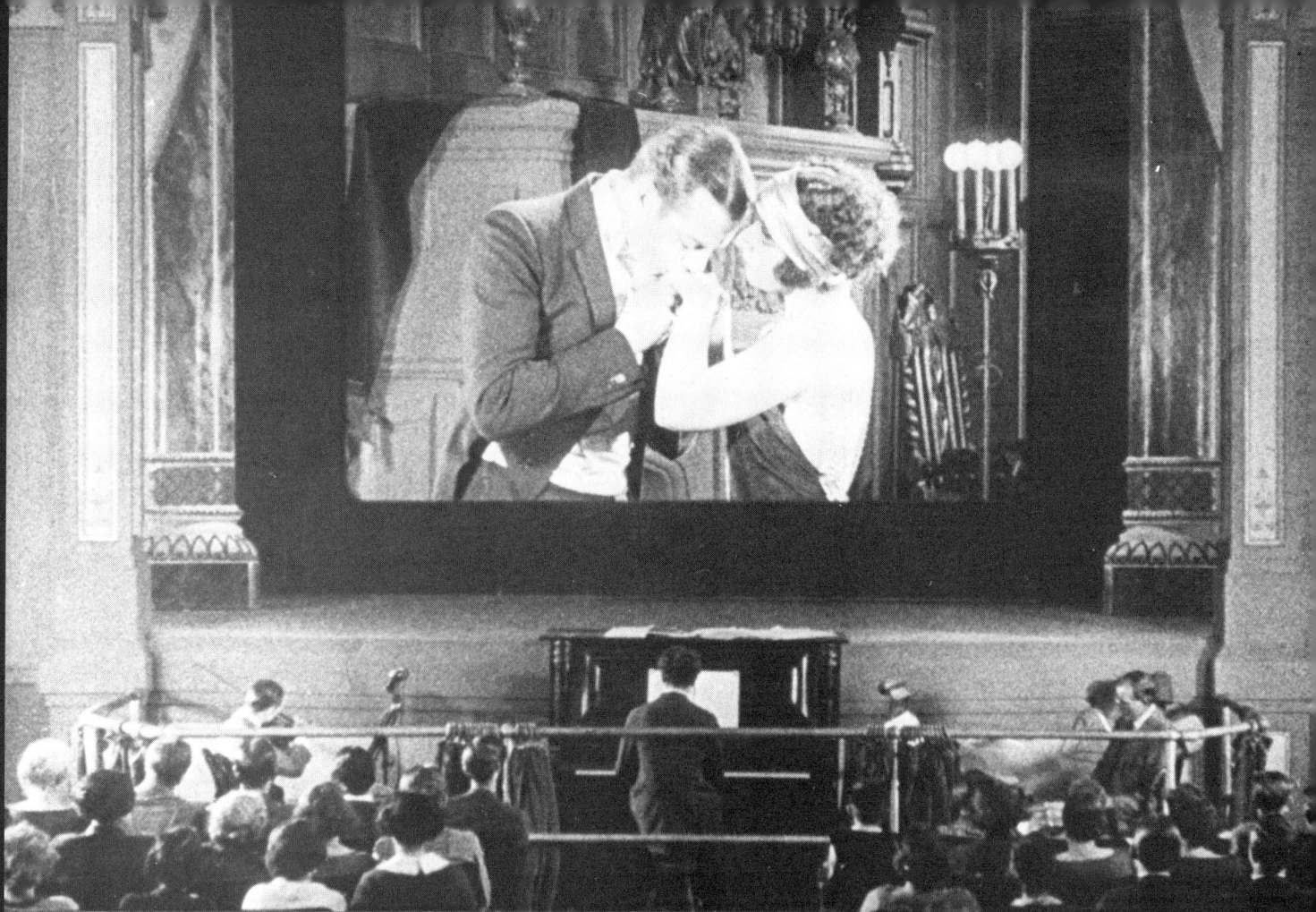

TRADE MARK

Metro Goldwyn Mayer

JOSEPH M. SCHENCK

Presents

BUSTER KEATON

IN

The Navigator

A Metro-Goldwyn Attraction

Rollo Treadway—
Heir to the Treadway
fortune—a living proof
that every family tree
must have its sap.

... *Buster Keaton*

"I think I'll get married."

"Today."

"We'll sail for Honolulu tomorrow on our honey-moon—get two tickets."

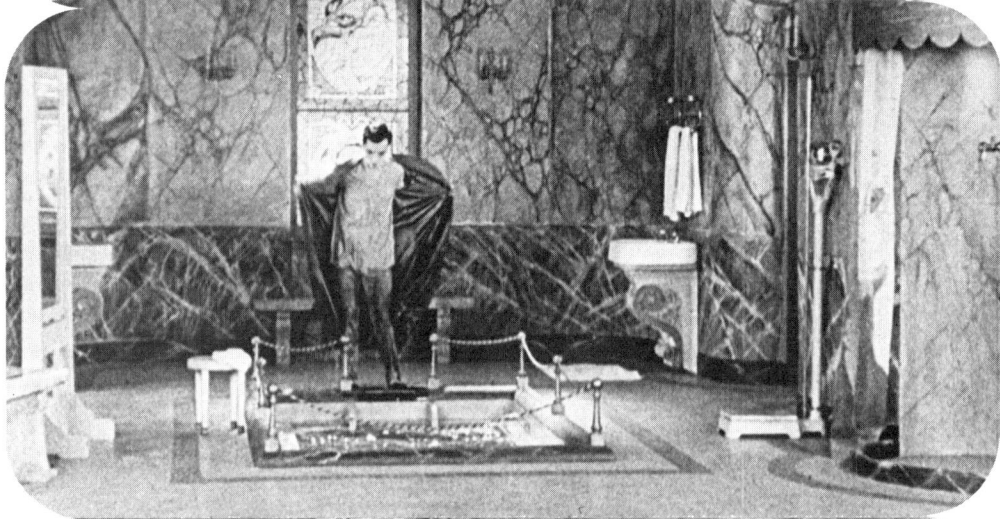

He had completed all arrangements — — except to notify the girl.

"Will you marry me?"

"Certainly not!"

"I think a long walk
would do me good."

Later: After his marriage proposal has been rejected Keaton decides to take a cruise in order to overcome his grief. He mistakenly boards a deserted ship which a group of sabateurs plan to cut loose from its moorings thus causing the ship to drift to sea to ultimate destruction.

Keaton's hopes for relaxation dissolve when he finally discovers that he is alone at sea on the abandoned ship.

And the situation is further complicated when he discovers that he really isn't alone. Rather, the shipowner's beautiful daughter finds herself accidently stranded on the ship. It's not until daylight that Keaton and the woman discover each other and set out to save themselves.

The following sequence details their attempt to catch up with a freighter which is steaming away from them. In order to attract the freighter's attention Keaton had raised a flag. On the advice of the shipowner's daughter he raised a yellow flag which she said was bright enough to get them noticed. But to the freighter it meant that their ship was quarantined.

"Try and catch them!"

"Hey! Wait a minute!"

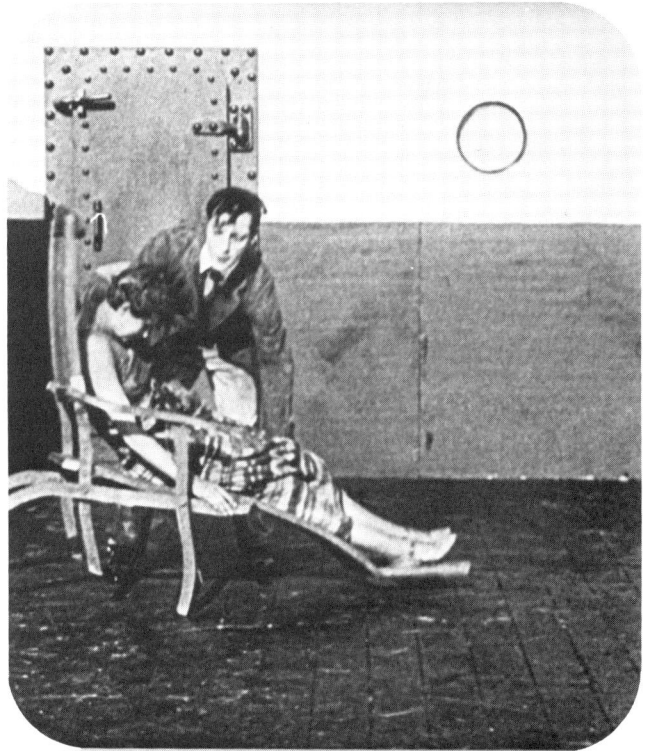

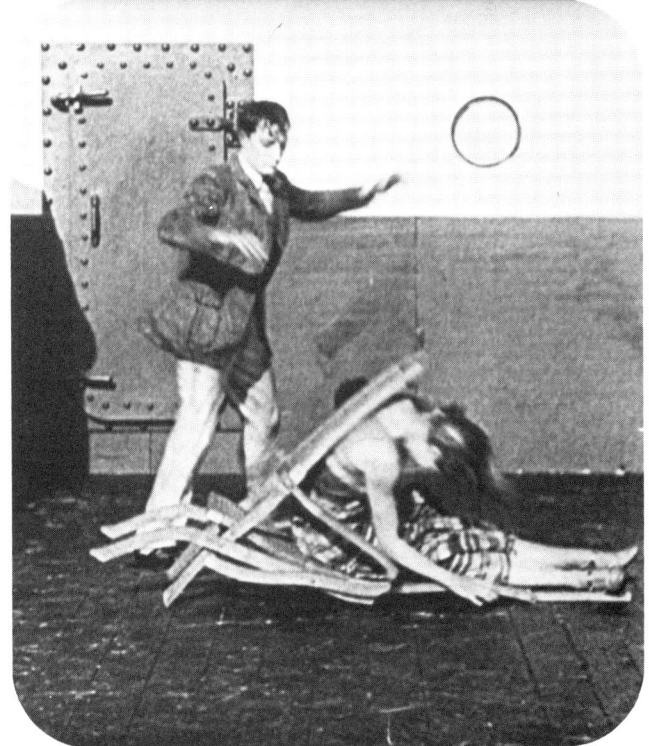

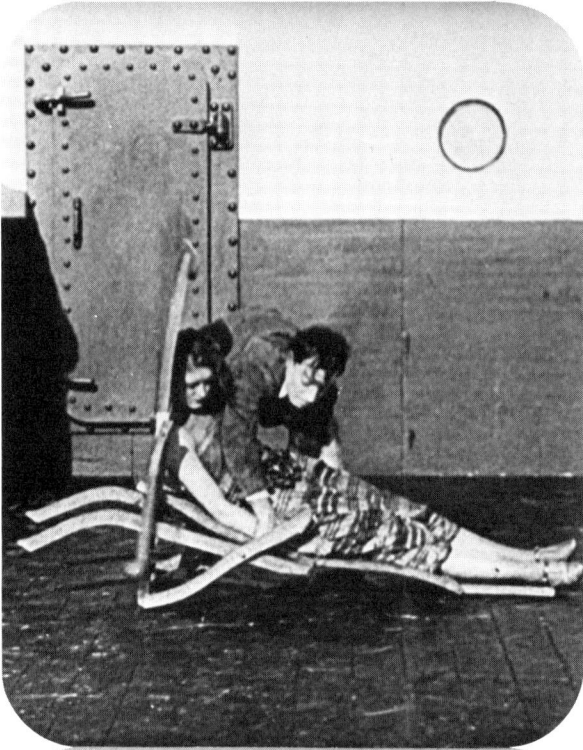

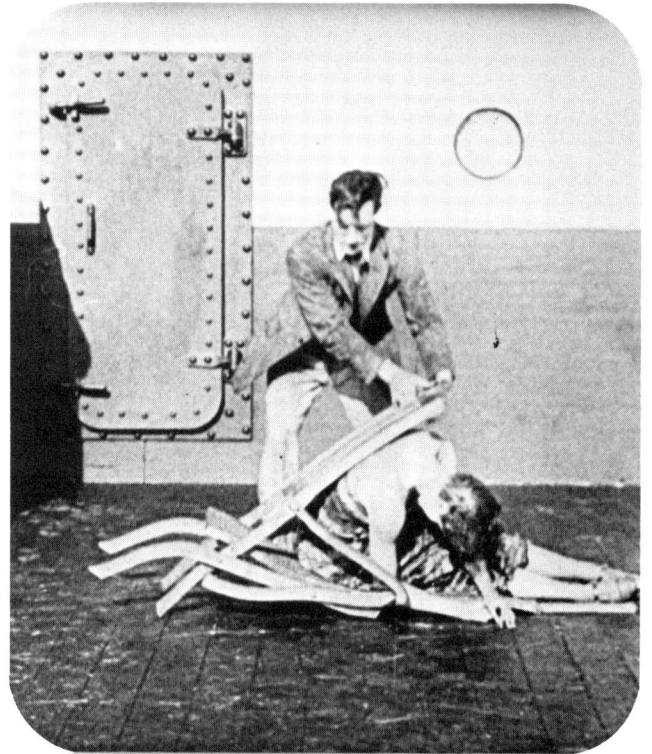

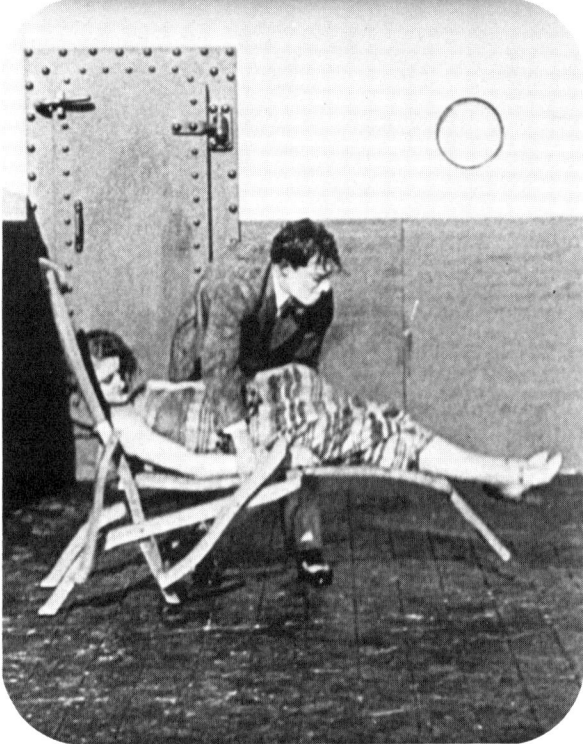

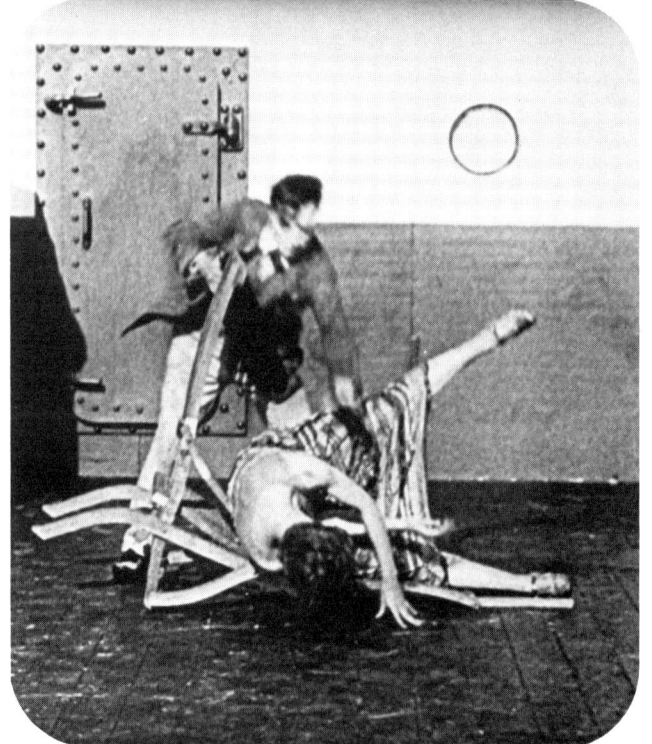

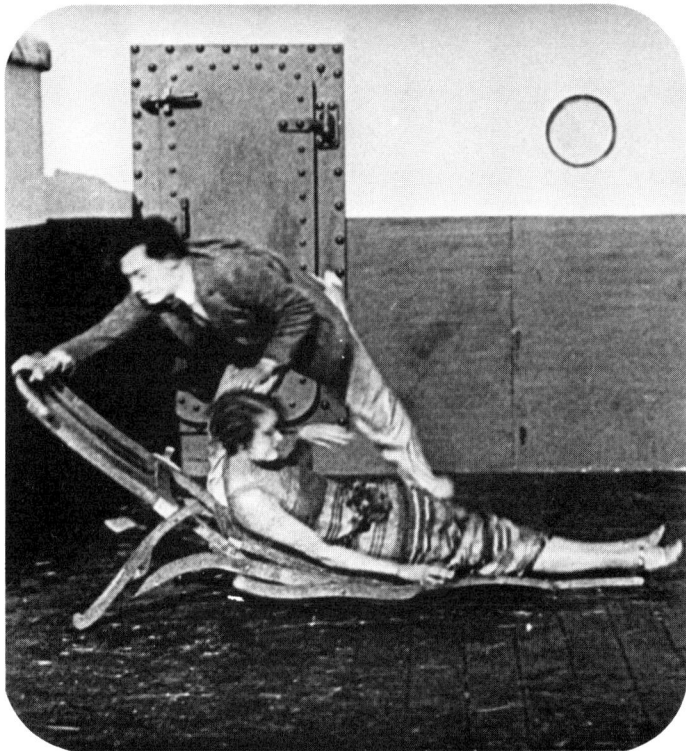

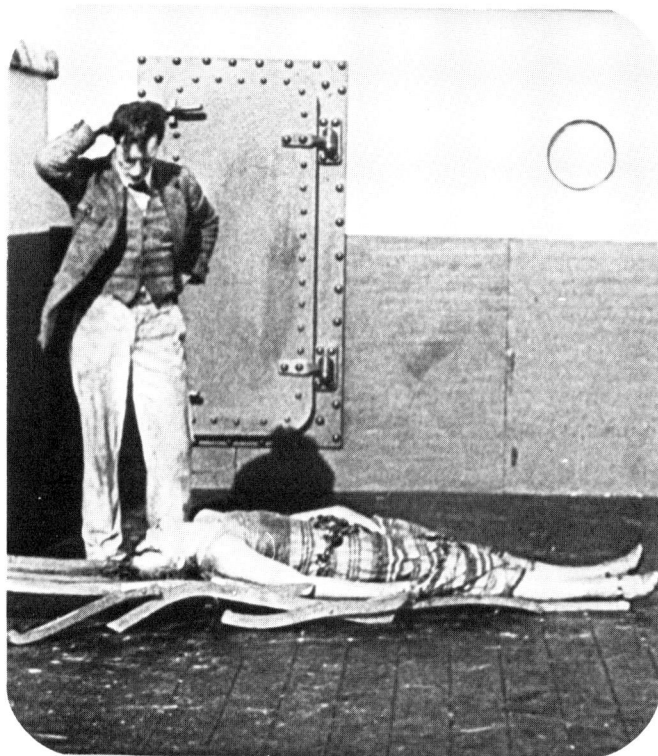

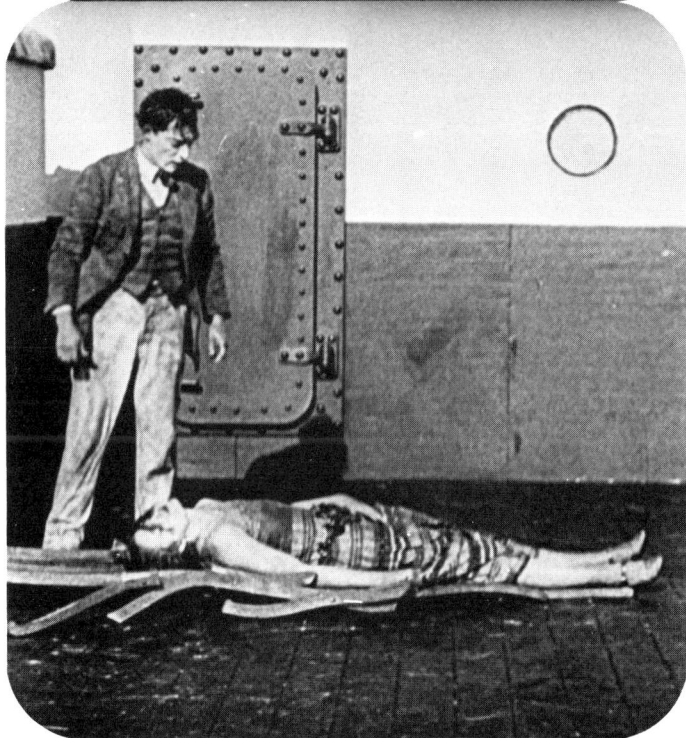

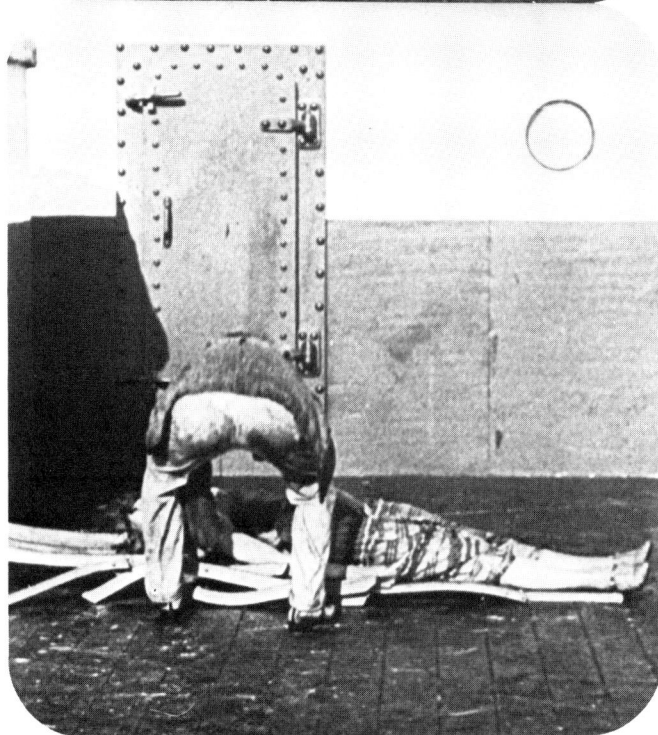

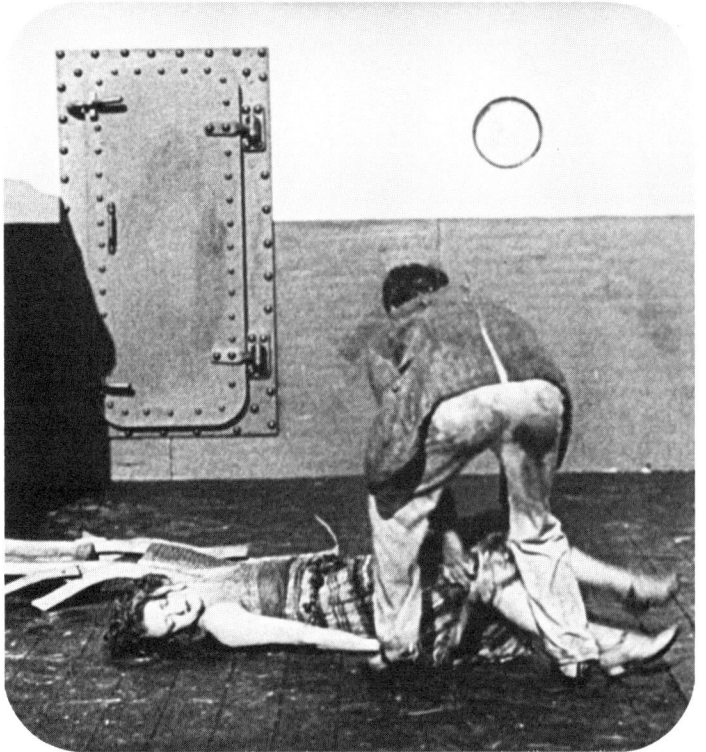

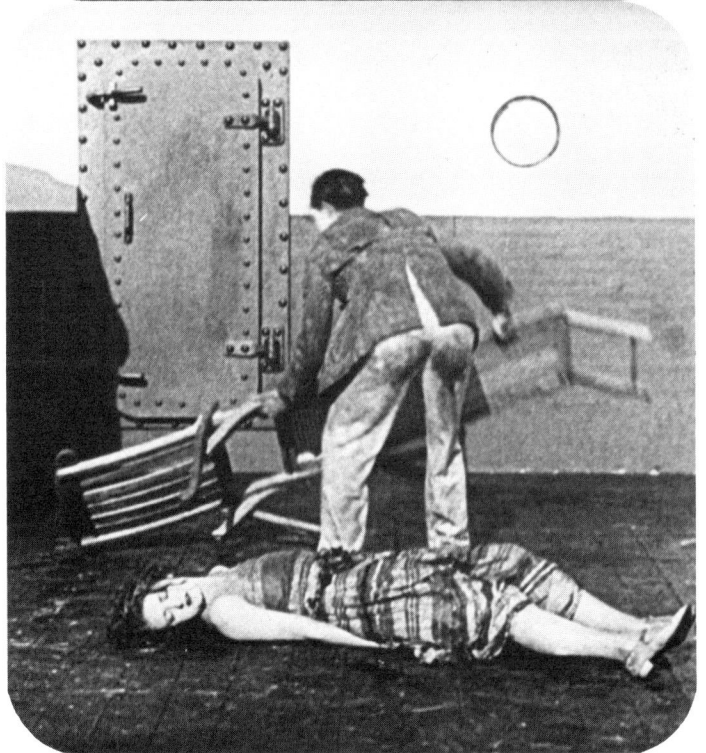

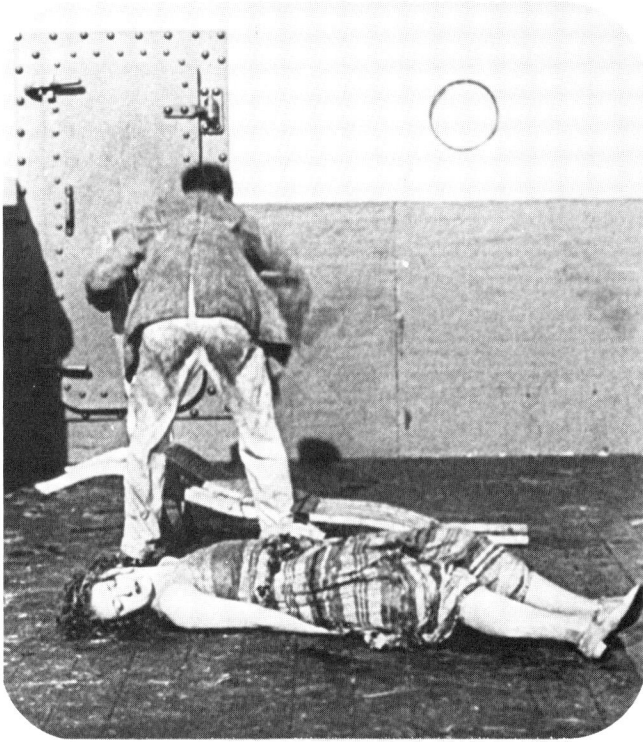

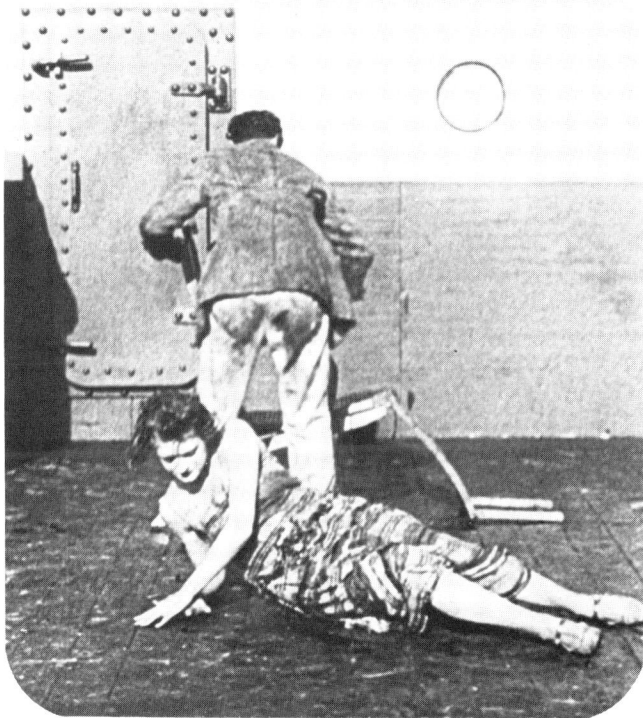

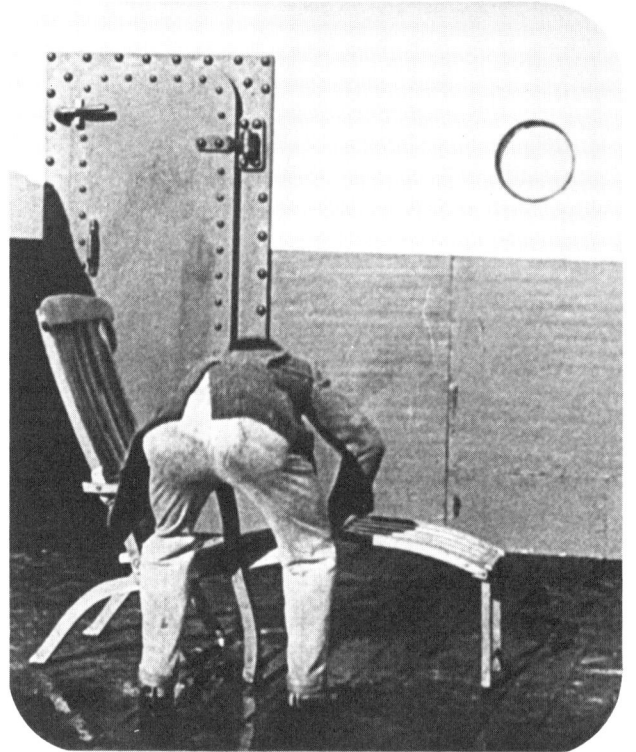

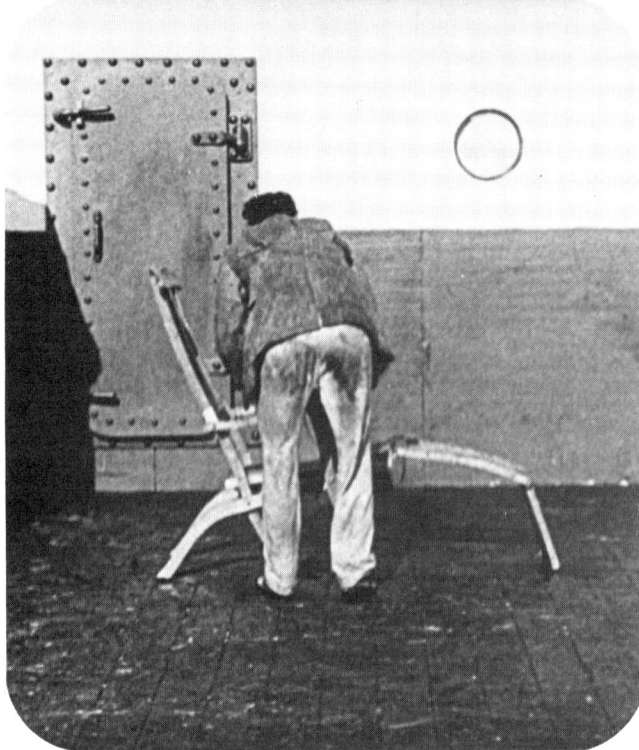

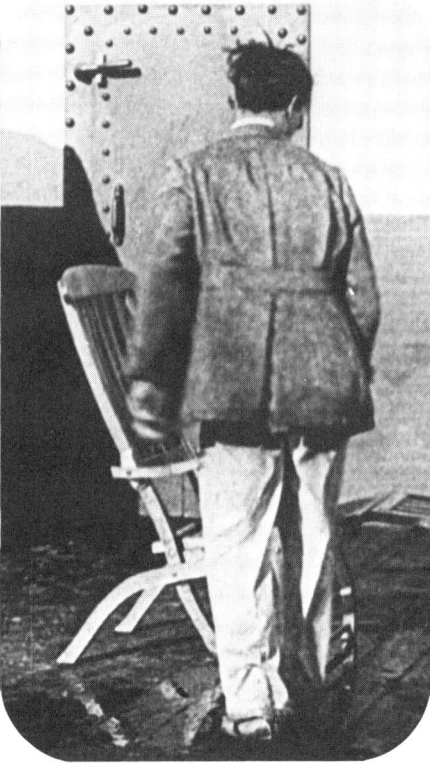

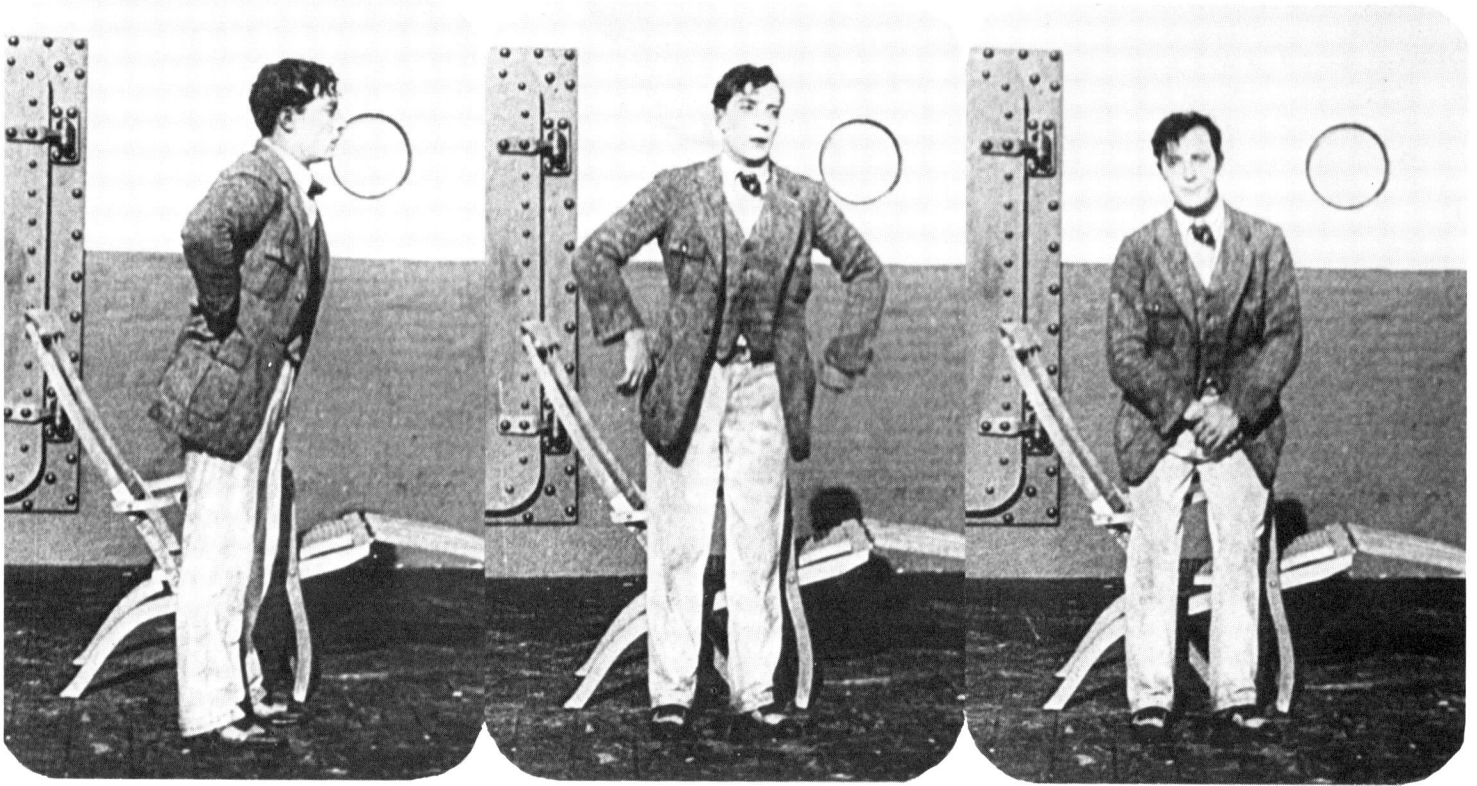

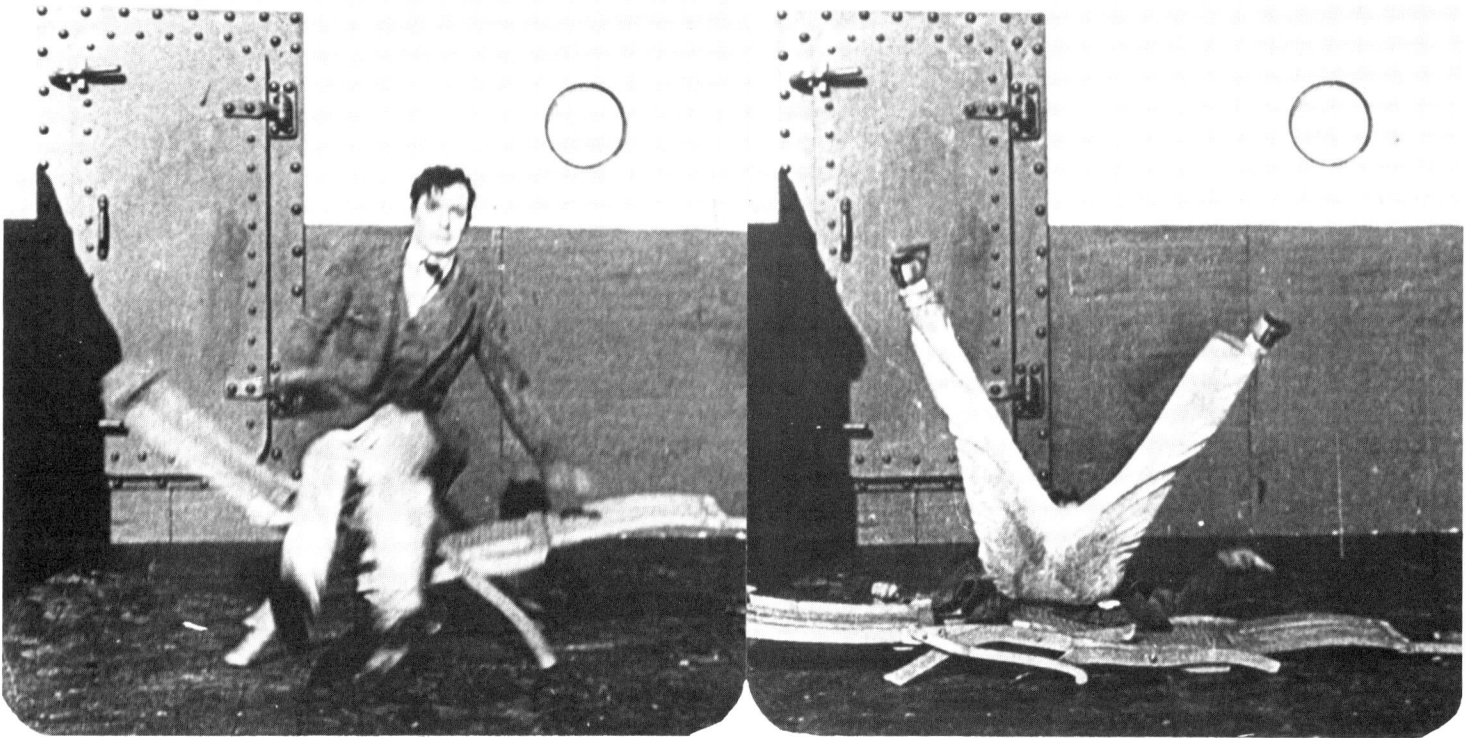

114

JOSEPH M. SCHENCK

presents

BUSTER KEATON

in

"GO WEST"

A Metro-Goldwyn Production

COPYRIGHT—BUSTER KEATON PRODUCTIONS, INC. 1925
COPYRIGHT RENEWED—LOEW'S INC. 1953

B·K

"GO WEST
YOUNG MAN
GO WEST"

HORACE GREELEY

Some people travel through life making friends where ever they go, while others— Just travel through life.

In a little town in Indiana, the social standing of a certain young man had kept him continuously on the move.

116

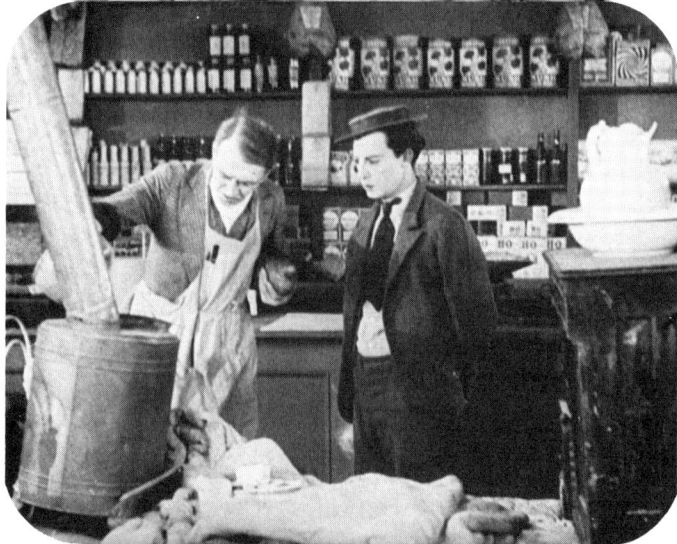

"I'll give you a dollar sixty five for the whole business."

"I've tried every place in town for a job, do you suppose there's any use asking you?"

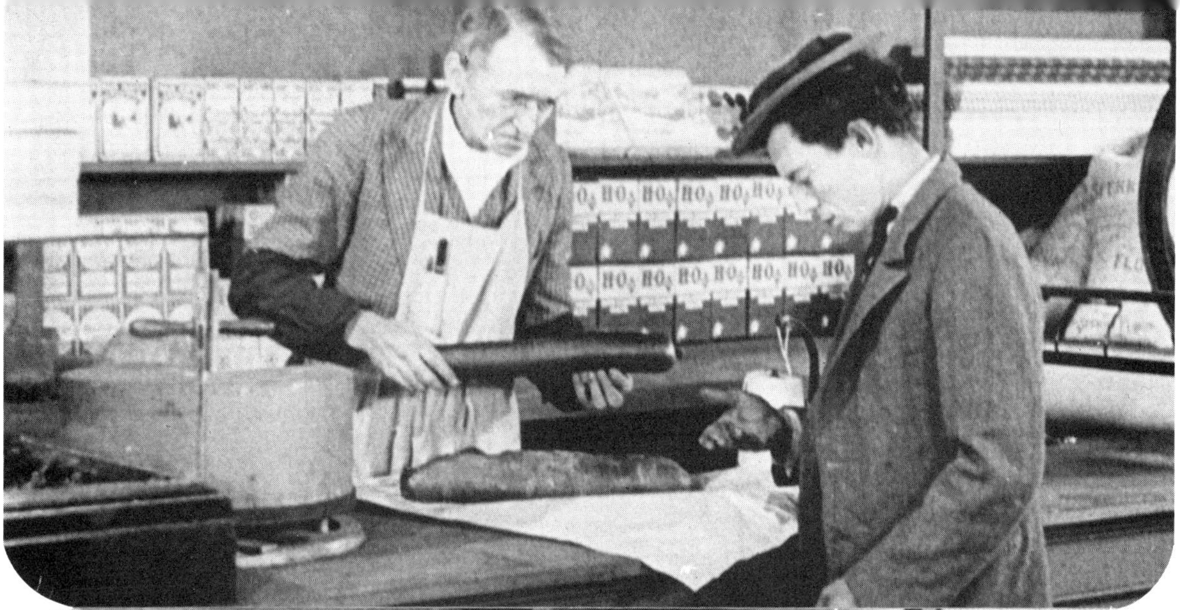
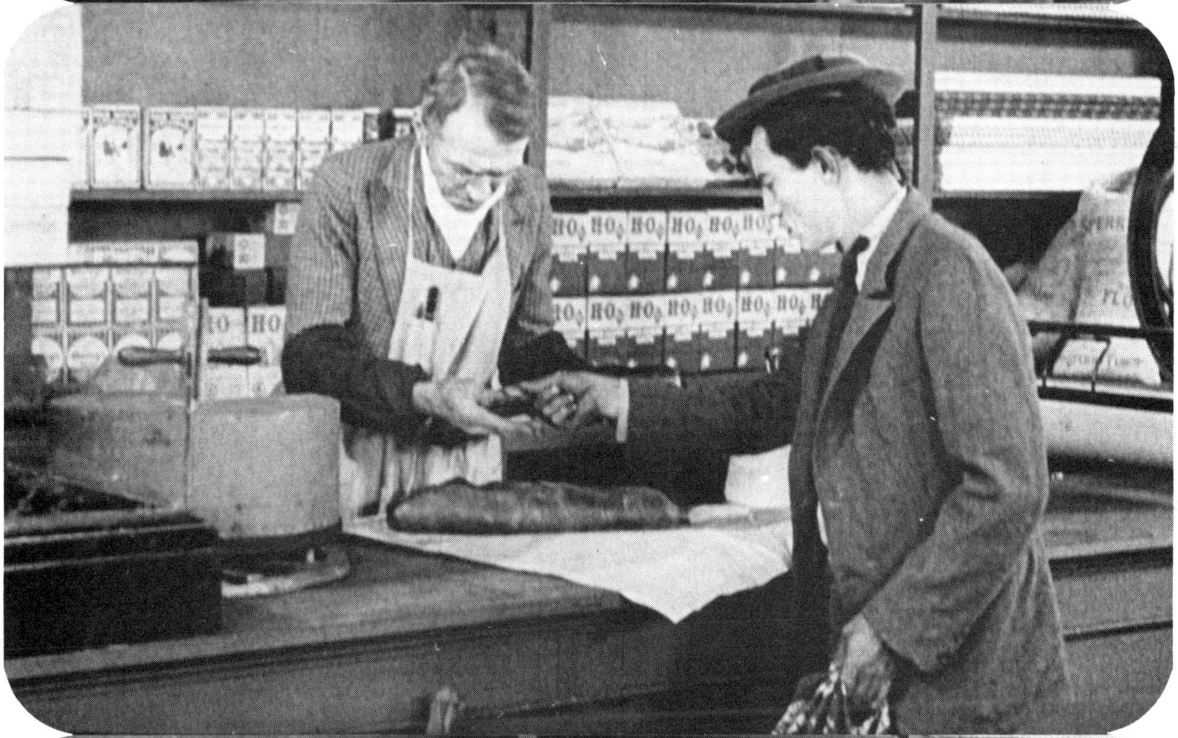
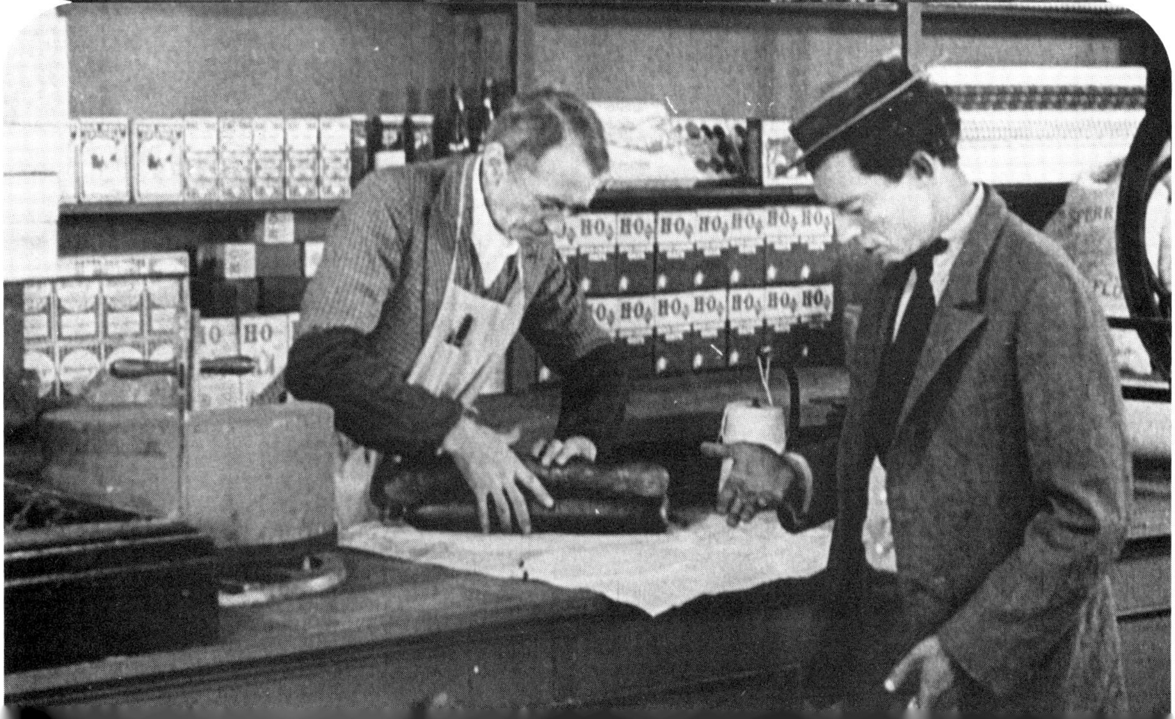

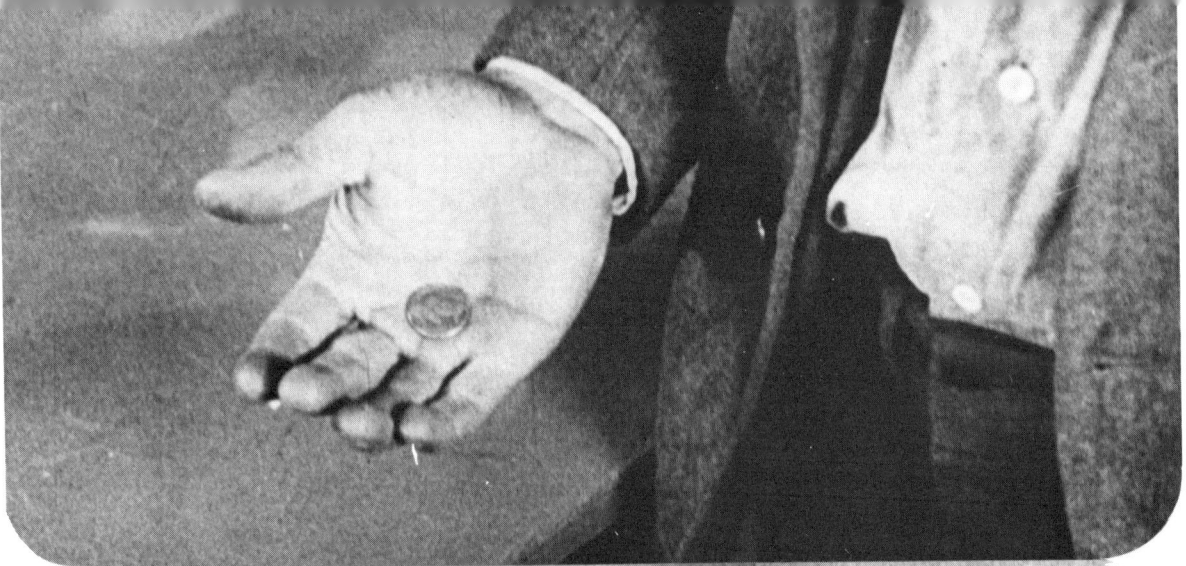

Having finally made his way out west Keaton must now convince everyone that he is a genuine cowboy. The following is his first encounter with a ranch owner and a cow.

"Do you need any
cowboys today?"

"I'm working here."

"You don't seem
to be."

JOSEPH M. SCHENCK

presents

Buster Keaton

IN

"SEVEN CHANCES"

A METRO-GOLDWYN PRODUCTION

The following sequence shows some of Keaton's ill-fated attempts to find a wife and the result of his partner placing an ad in the local newspaper.

Keaton's grandfather has left him $7 million on condition that he be married by 7 PM on his twenty-seventh birthday. By the time the will is read it already is the day of Keaton's twenty-seventh birthday and he is still single.

He hastily runs off to see his girlfriend who refuses to marry him after he bungles the proposal. In desperation Keaton and his partners set out to find a marriage partner.

159

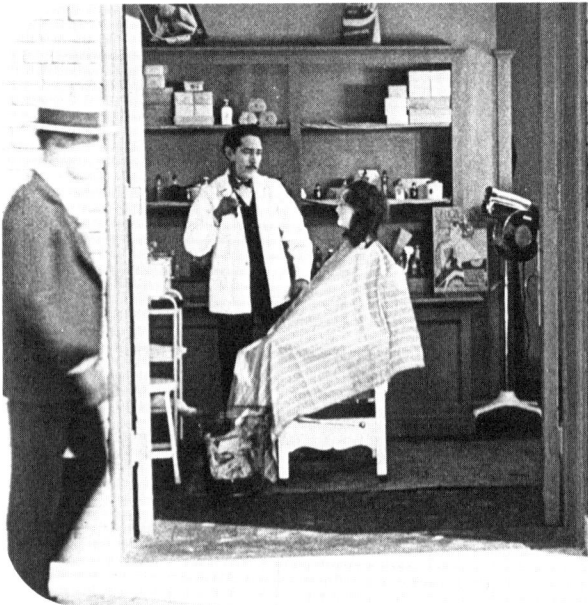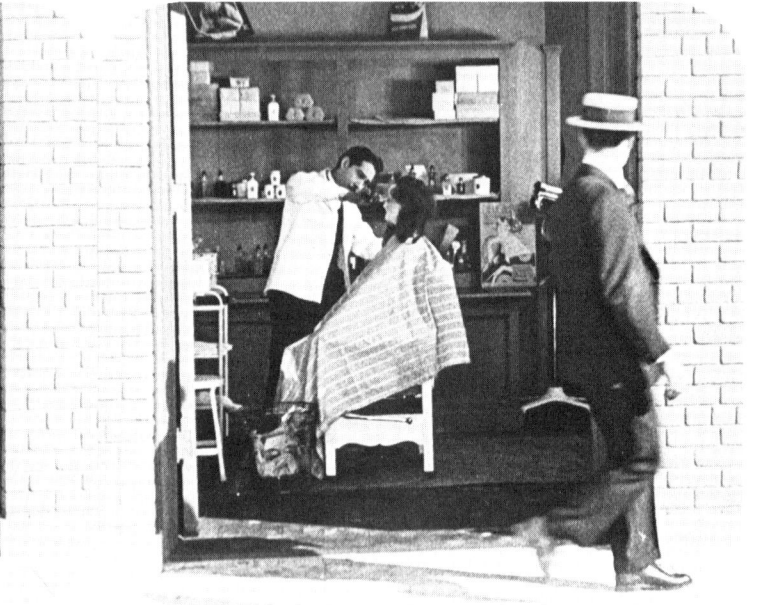
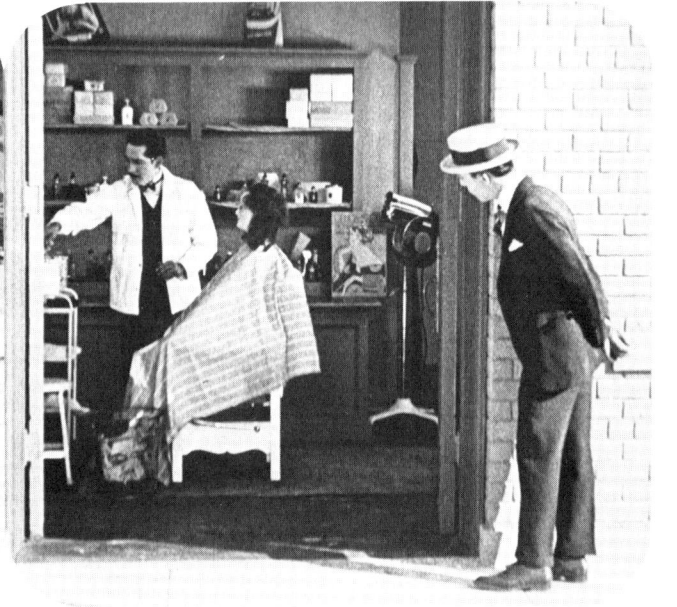

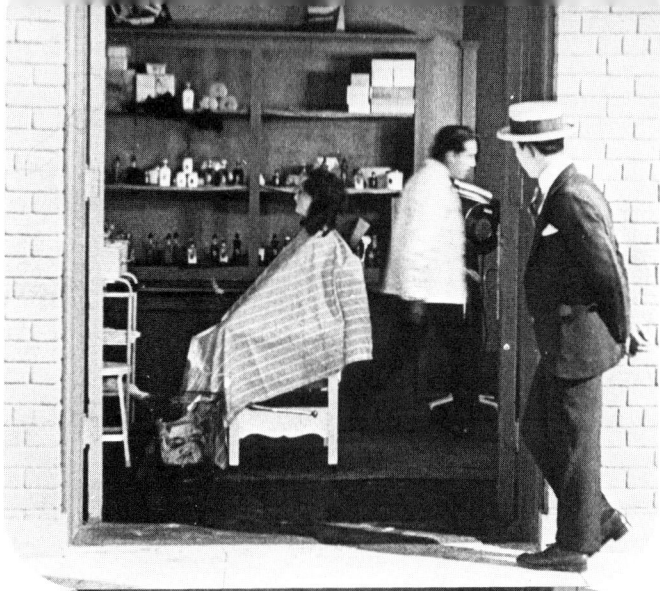

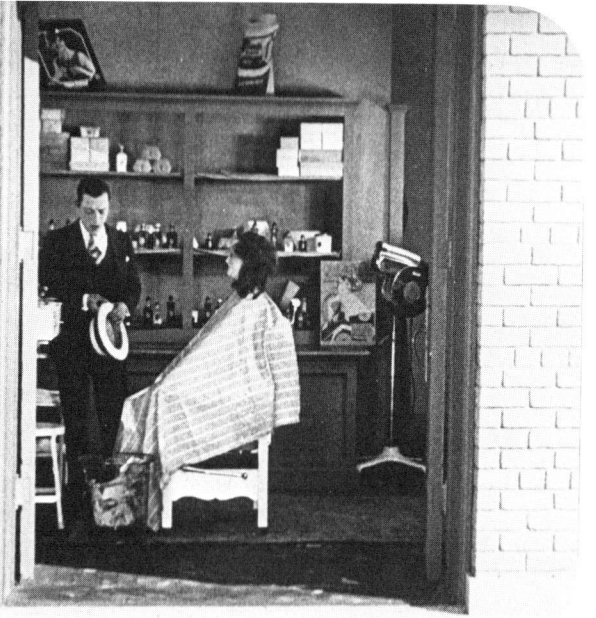

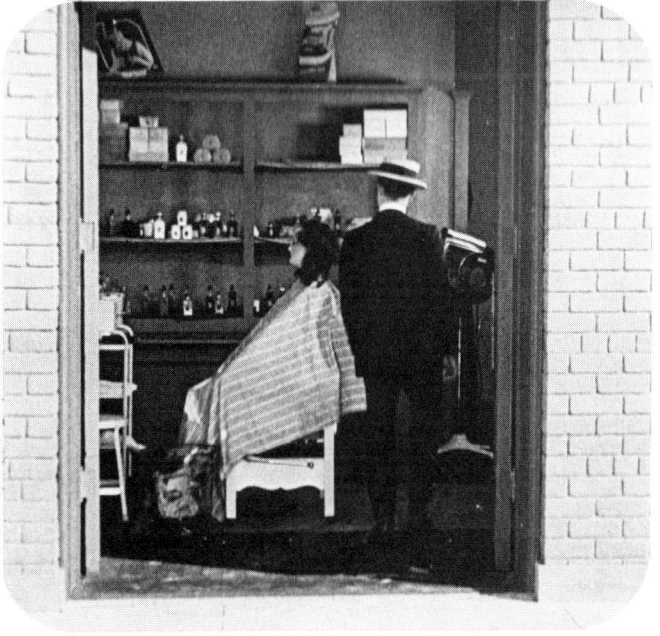

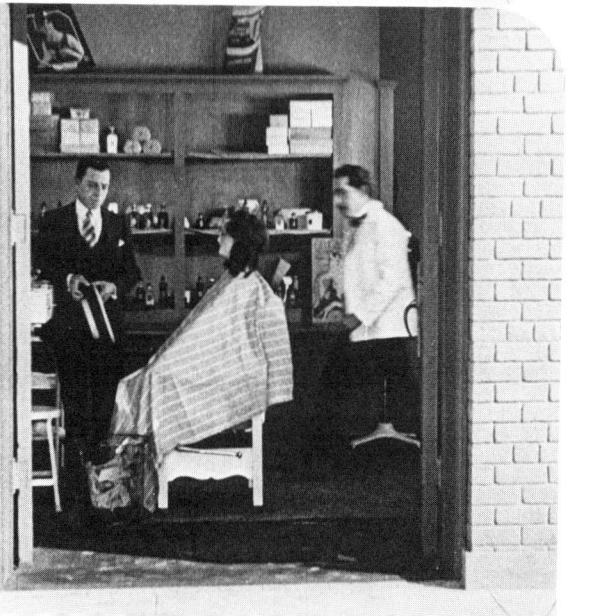

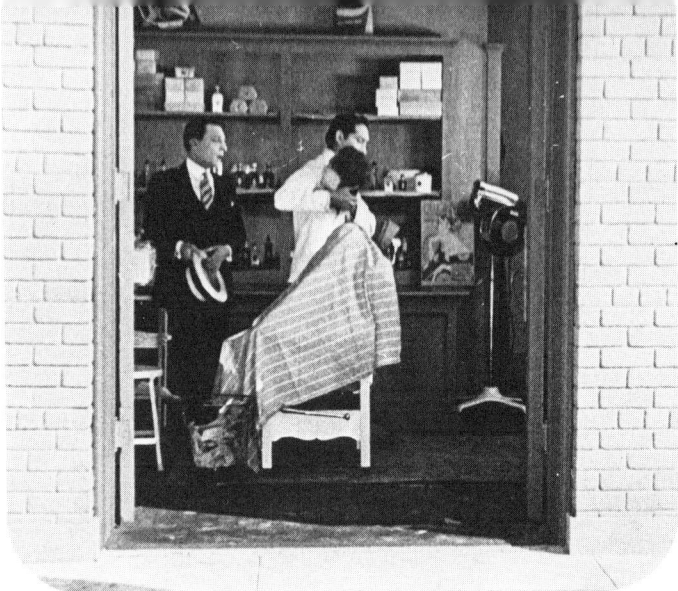

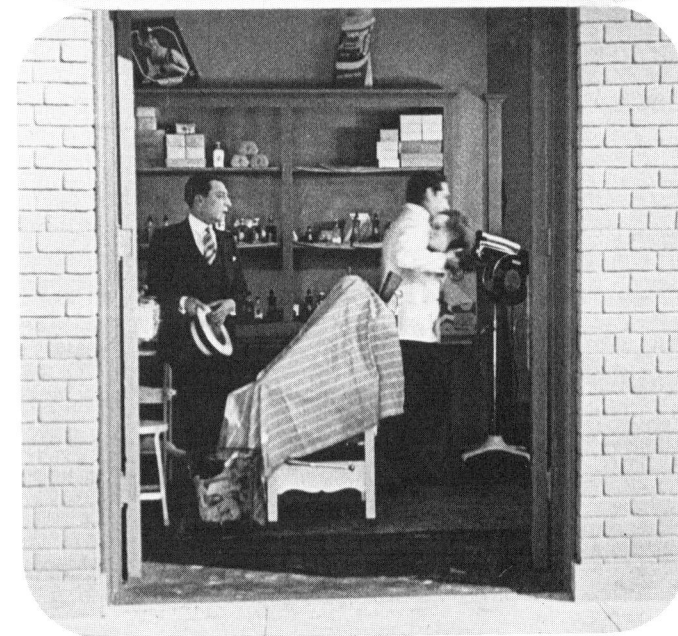

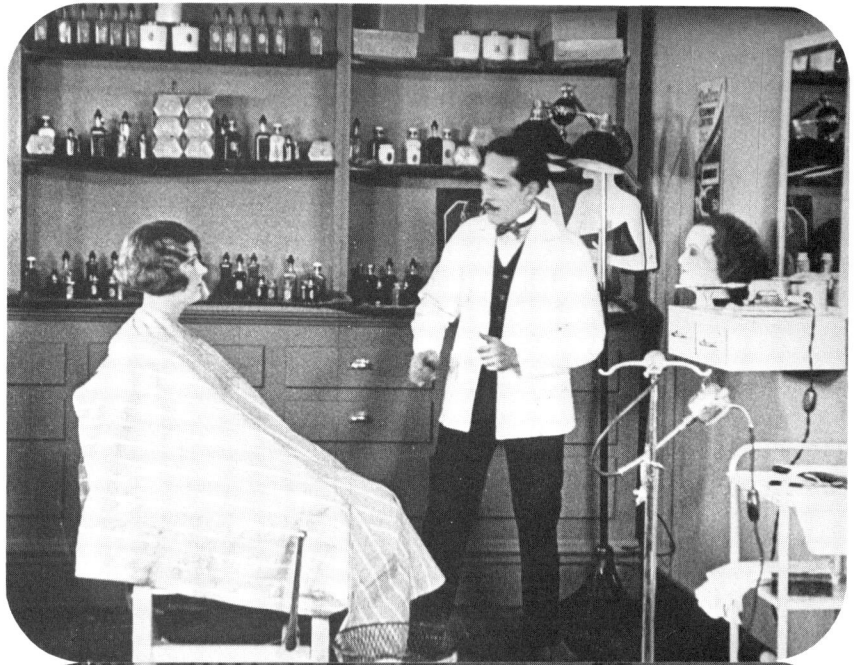

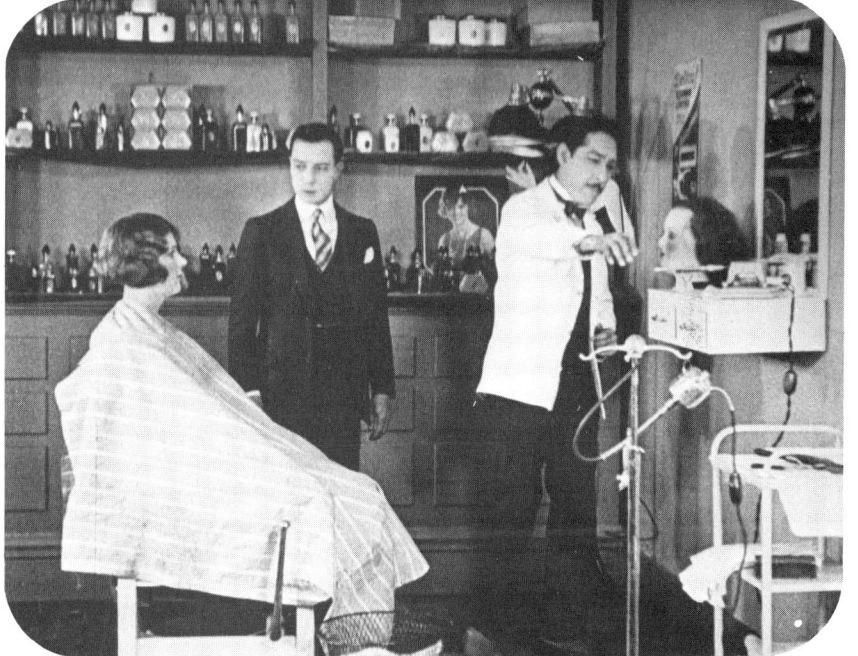

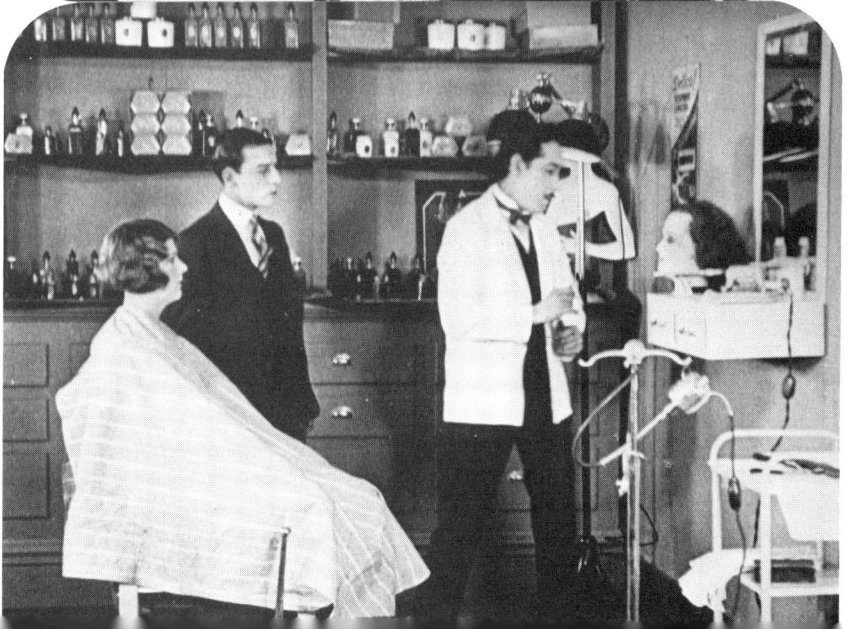

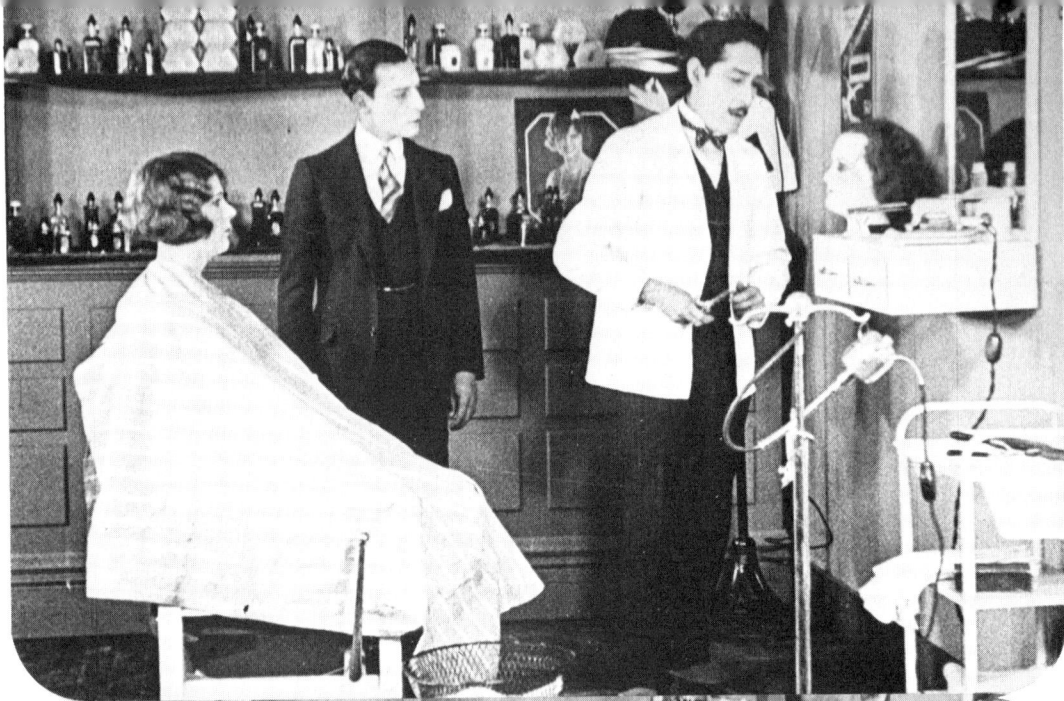

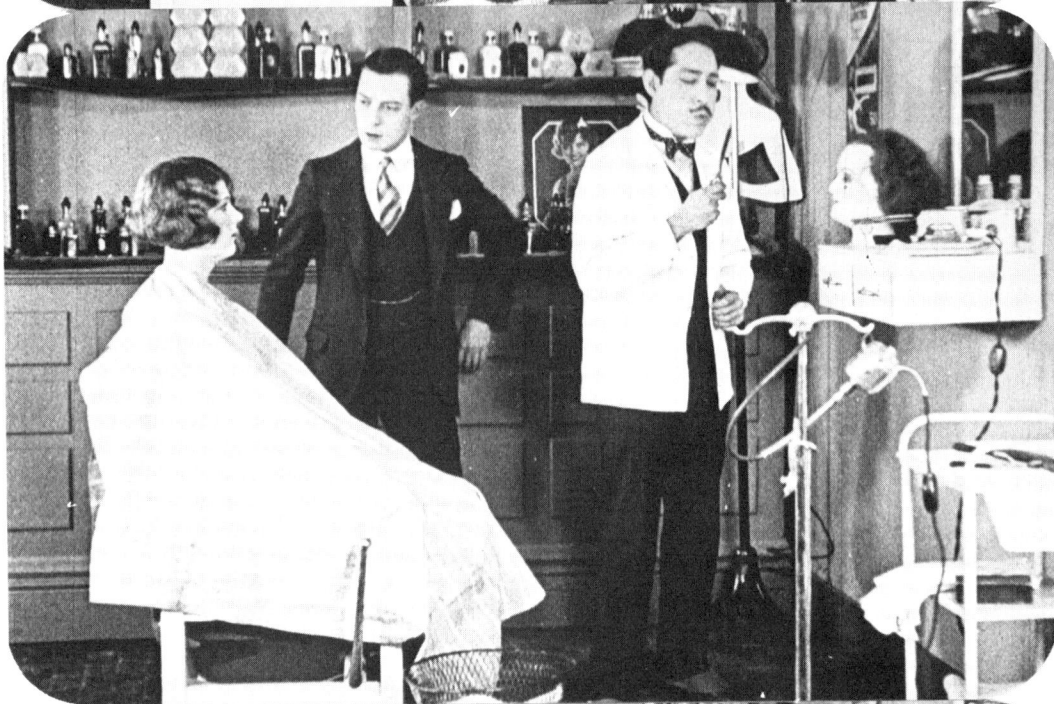

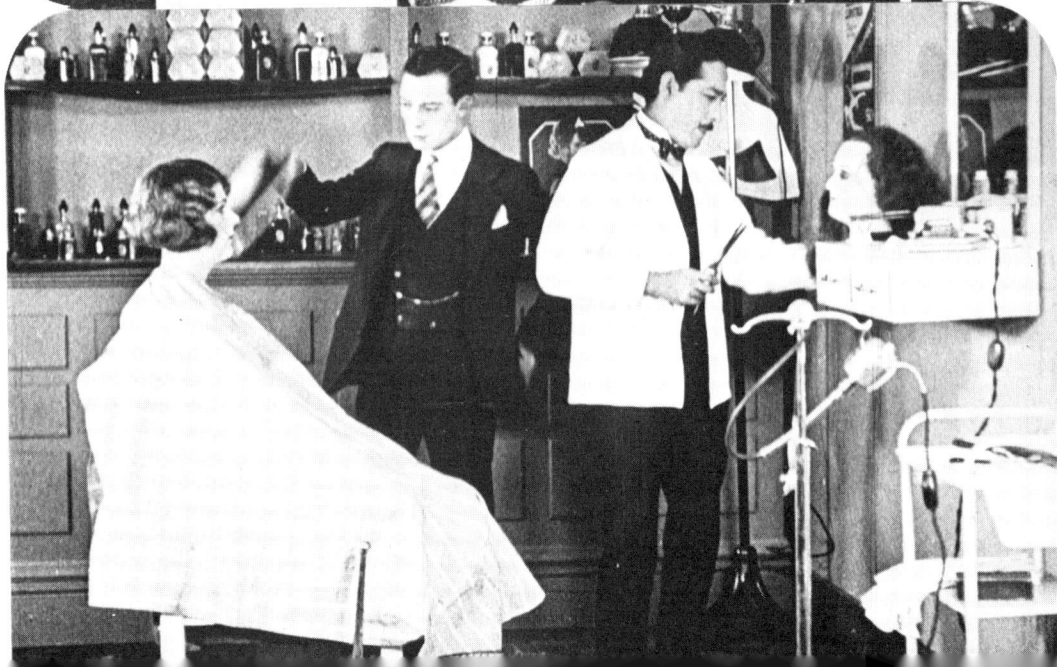

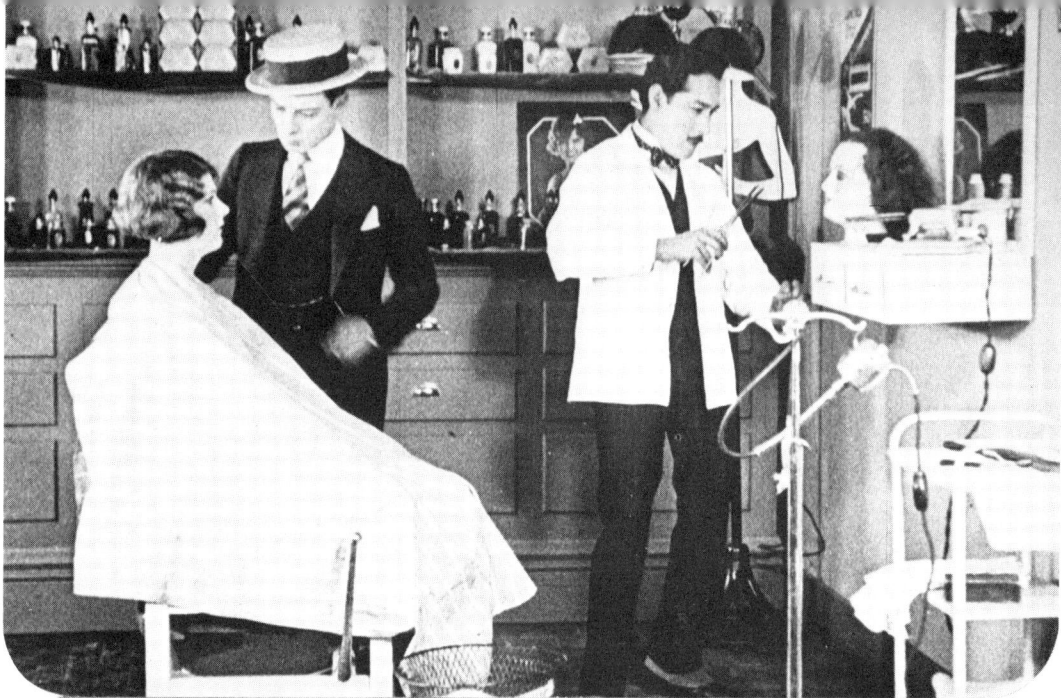
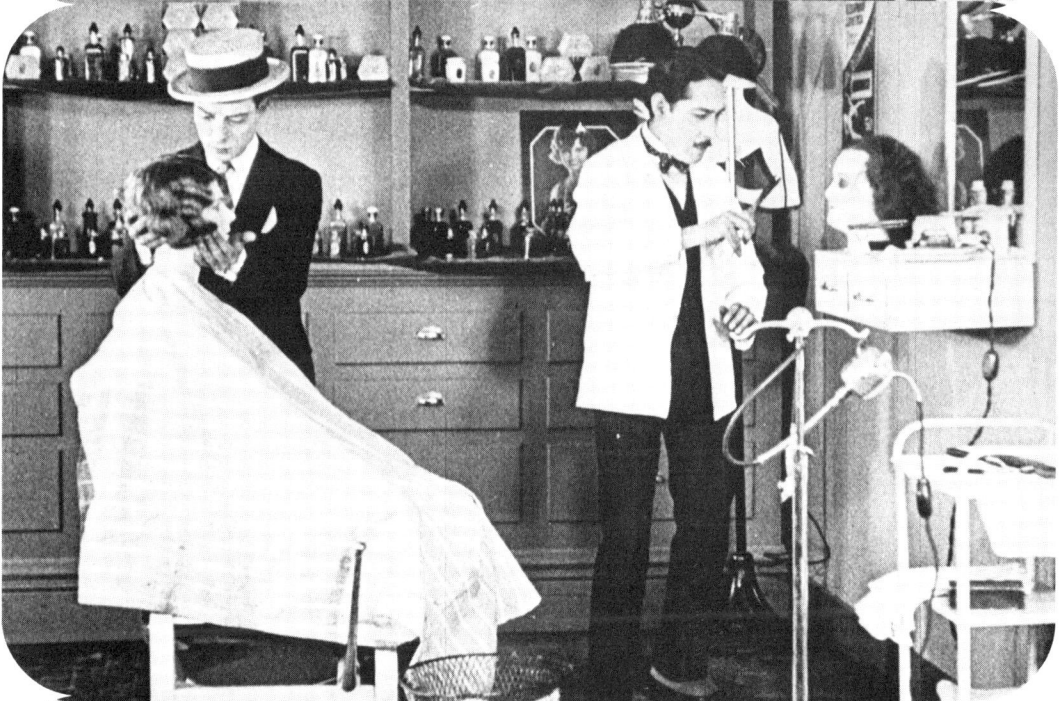
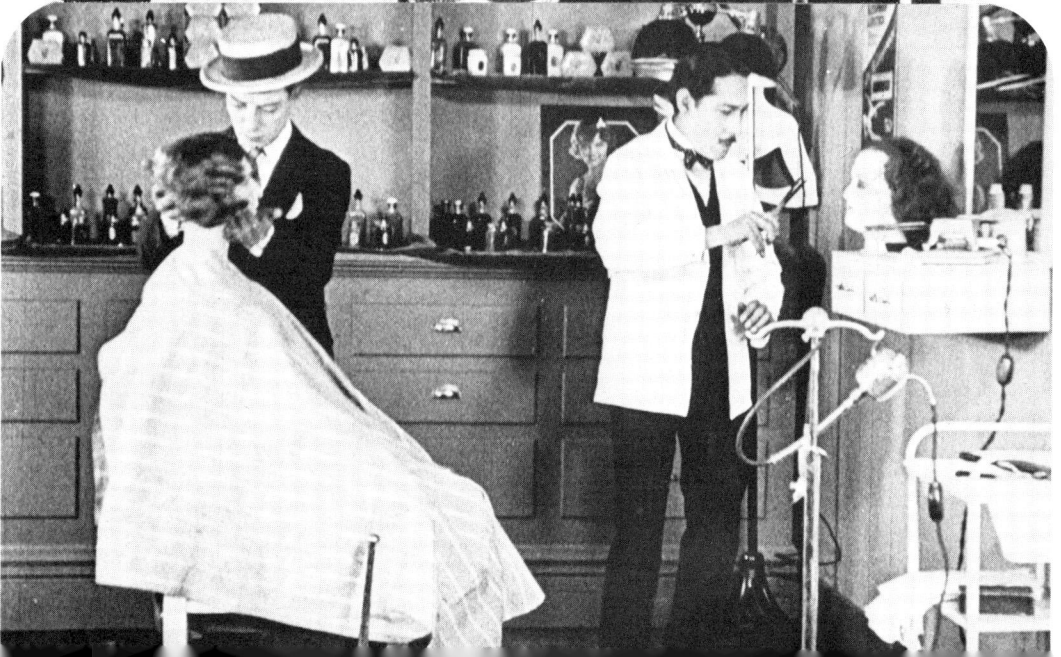

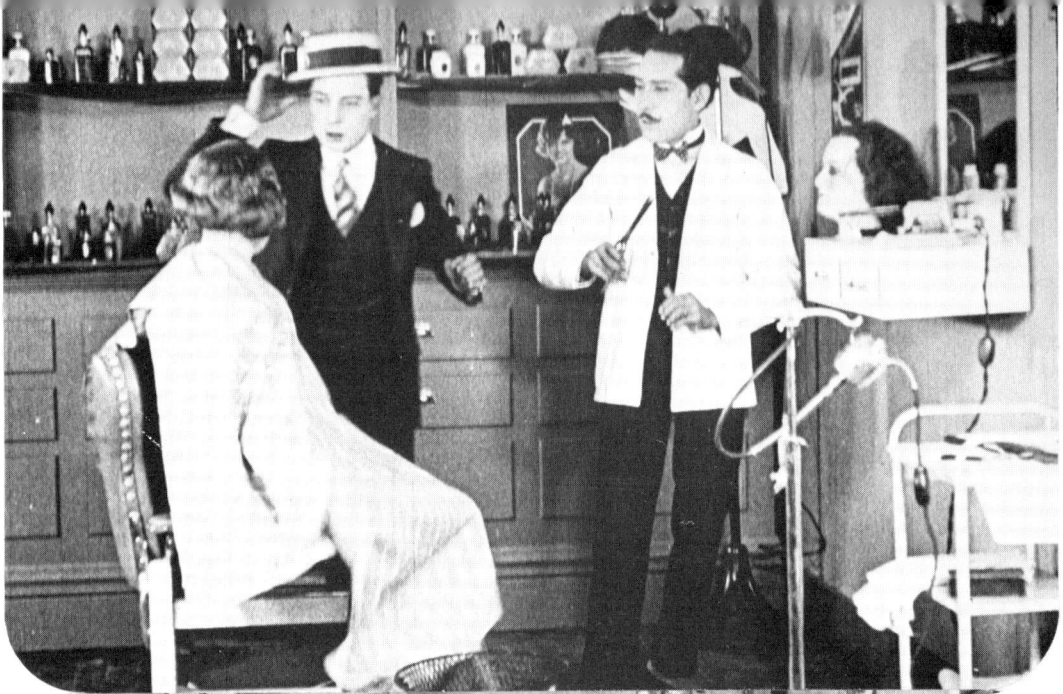

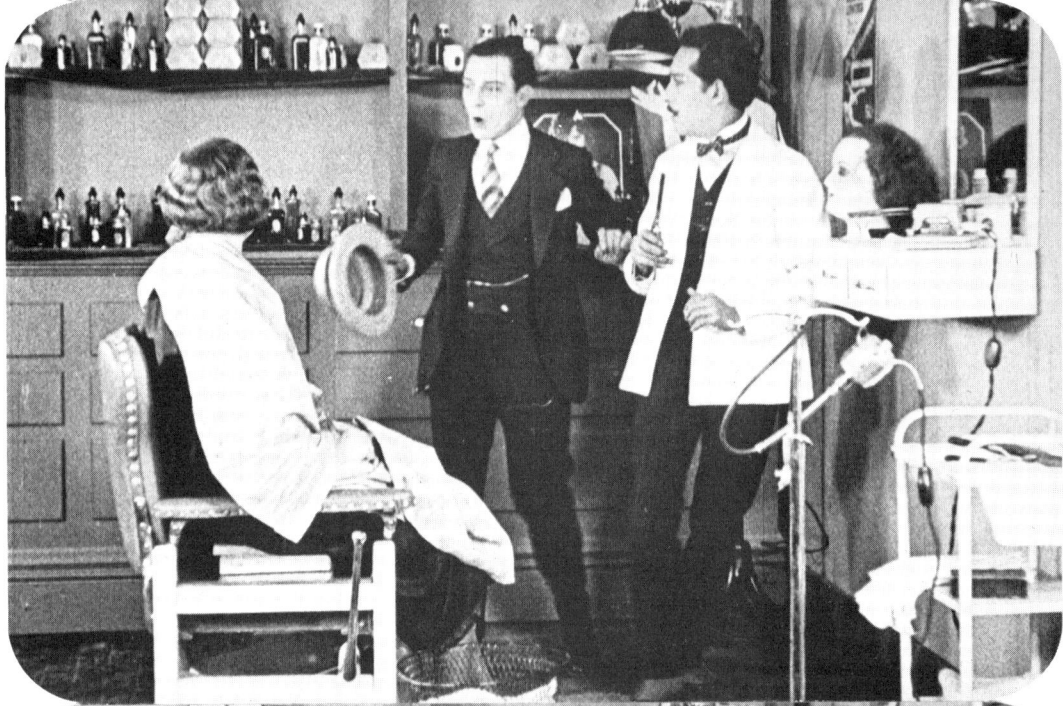

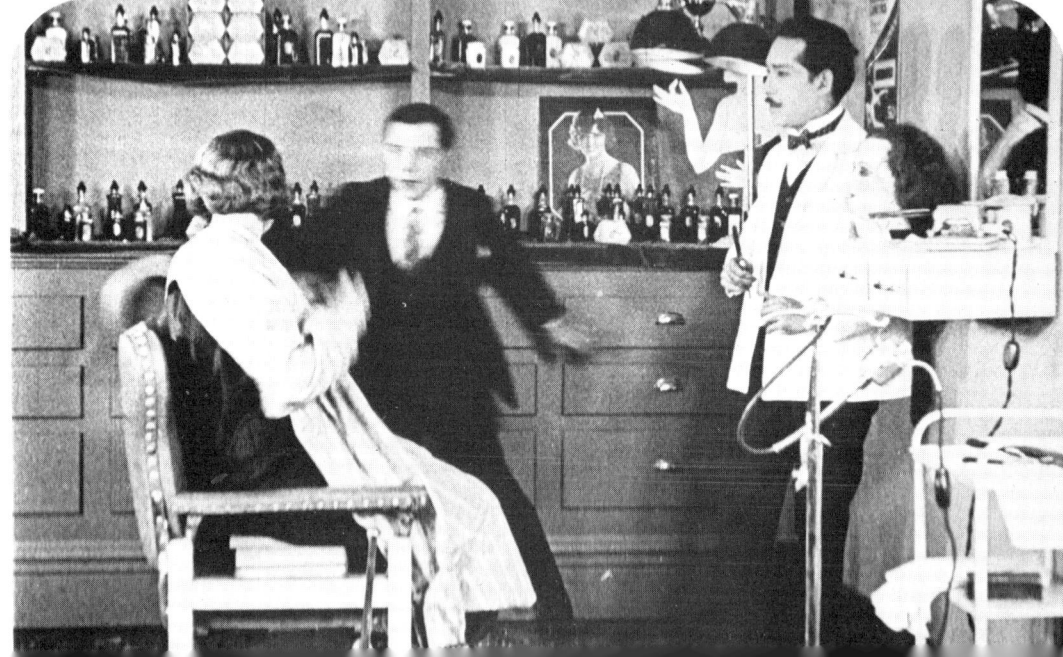

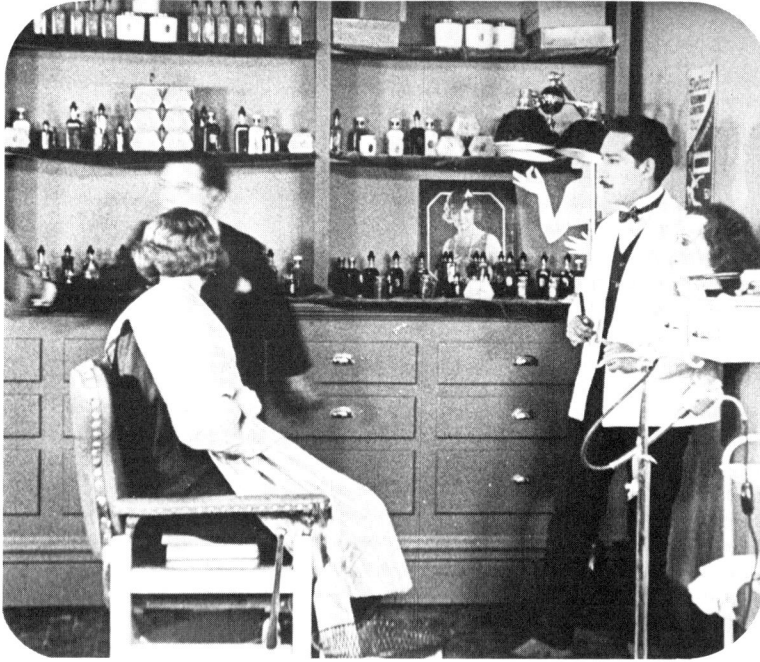 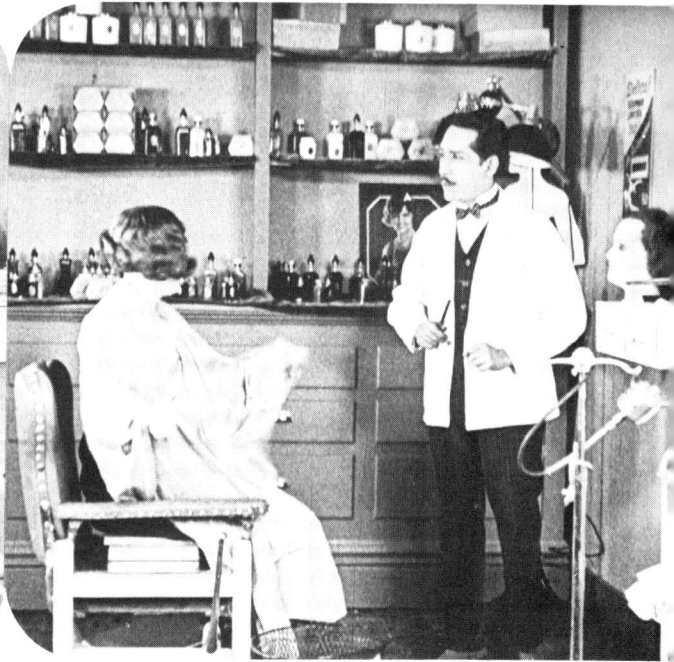

★ ★ ★ ★

WANTED, A BRIDE

James Shannon, Prominent Young Broker Falls Heir to $7,000,000 If He Is Married Today

ALL HE NEEDS IS A BRIDE

Girl Who Appears at Broad Street Church In Bridal Costume By 5 O'Clock Will Be the Lucky Winner

One of the most unique wills ever filed for probate was recorded yesterday in the court of deeds by Caleb Rathbone, executor for the estate of the late Jabez Shannon. By the codicil of the will James Shannon, prominent young broker of the firm of Meekin & Shannon becomes sole heir of his grand father's vast estate providing he is married on his twenty-seventh birthday. Shannon's birthday happens to be today and if he succeeds in securing a bride before the time designated by the terms of the will, he will have very little time to choose his wife

JAMES SHANNON, WHO MAY BE WORTH $7,000,000 BY 7 P. M.

PROGRAM OF EVENTS	JUST AROUND THE CORNER

By the time Jimmie had reached the church, he had proposed to everything in skirts, including a Scotchman.

In selling this ticket and checking
baggage hereon, the selling carrier acts
only as agent and is not responsible
beyond its own line.

22	23	24
25	26	27
28	29	30
X	X	31

1900 AND

23	24	25
26	27	28
29	30	31

(Signature of Original Purchaser)

NIAGARA FALLS

(Destination)

Good only with coupons of this Company's issue
attached hereto.

Form_____ No. _____

orm_____ No. _____

rm_____ No. _____

_____ No. _____

Form 8401

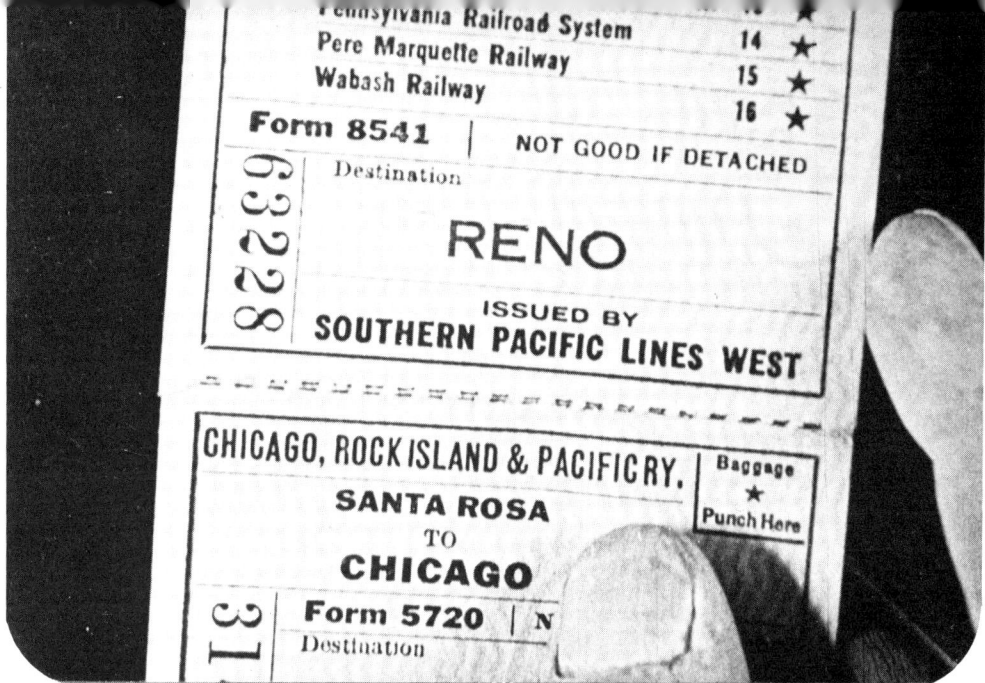

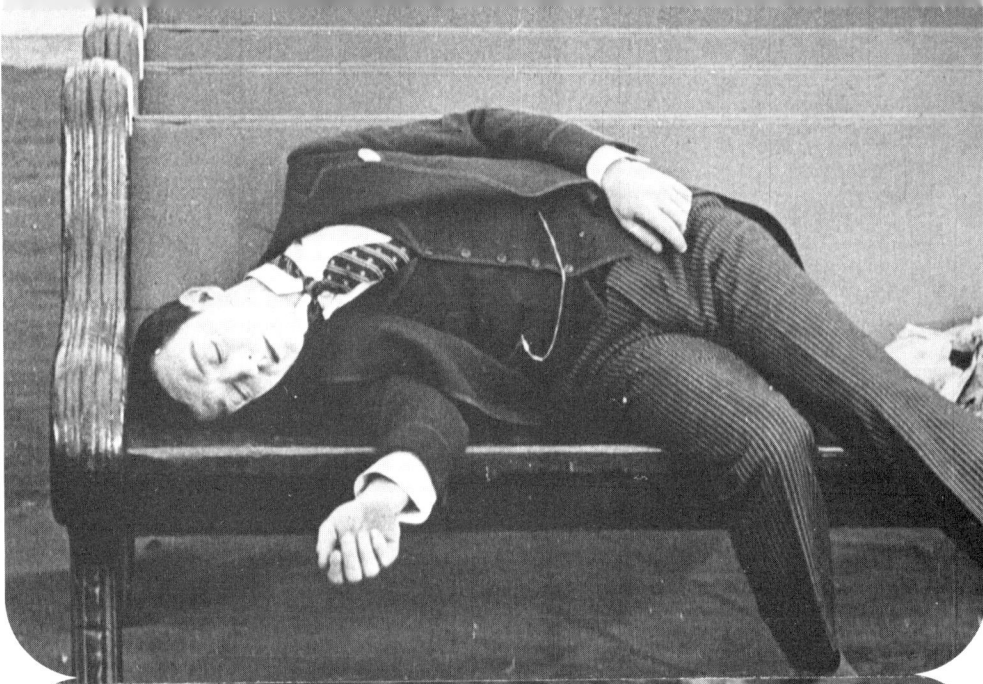

Joseph M. Schenck
PRESENTS
BUSTER KEATON
IN
"THE GENERAL"
A UNITED ARTISTS PRODUCTION

Keaton portrays a Southern railroad engineer who has been rejected for service in the Southern Army at the outset of the Civil War. The recruiting officers felt that Keaton would be more valuable to the South's war cause if he remained at the helm of his locomotive, "The General."

Of course, only the audience realizes this. To his girlfriend and her family Keaton appears to be a coward who refused to join the Southern cause. Only after his train is hijacked and Keaton sets out to catch up with the Northern spies who have plans to cut off the Southern Army's supply lines does Keaton regain his honor.

The following sequence has "The General" being hijacked along with Keaton's sweetheart. Only about a quarter of the chase sequence is recreated here but it is enough to give you a good idea of Keaton's masterful timing. And, keep in mind that Keaton always performed all of his own stunts.

'Big Shanty. Twenty minutes for dinner.'

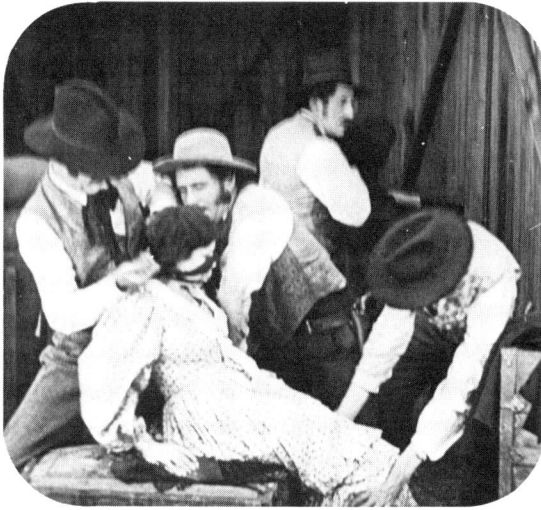

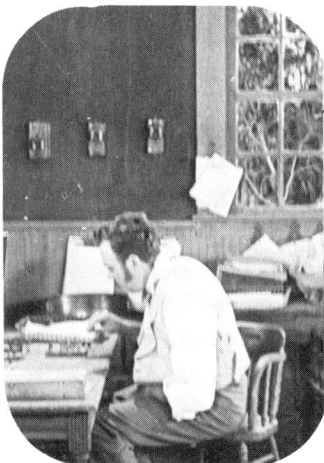

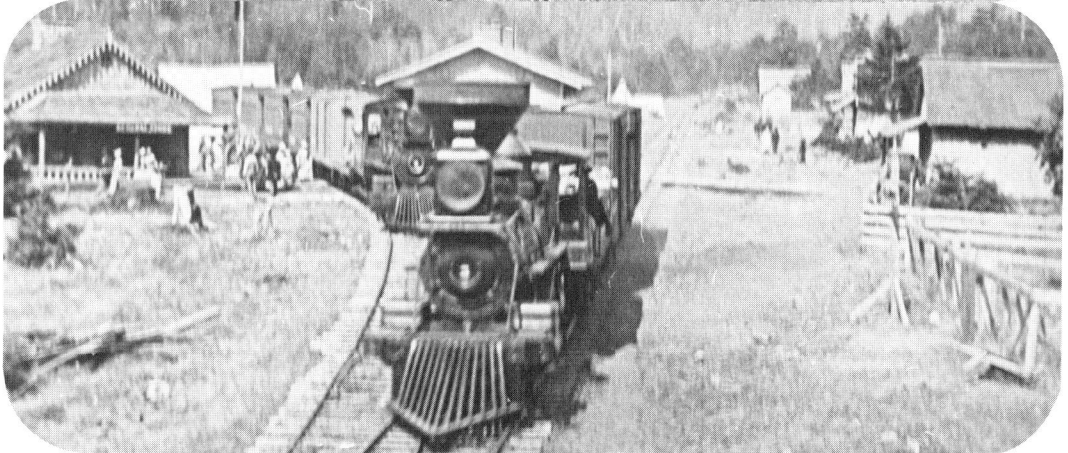

'Three men stole my General. I think they are deserters.'

'Why not stop and fight them?'

'I'm afraid they have us greatly outnumbered.'

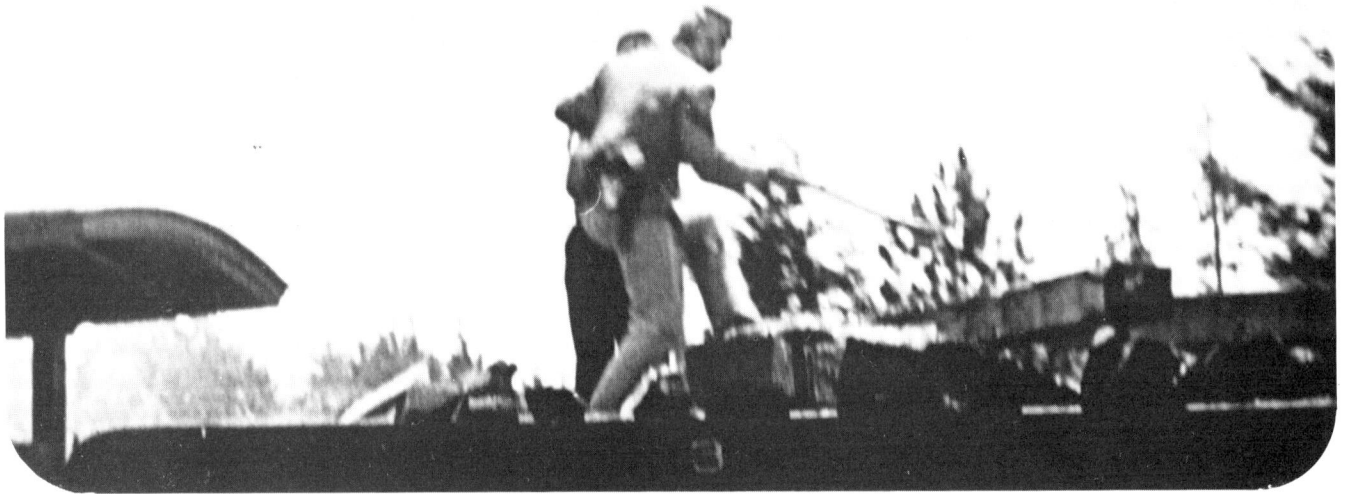

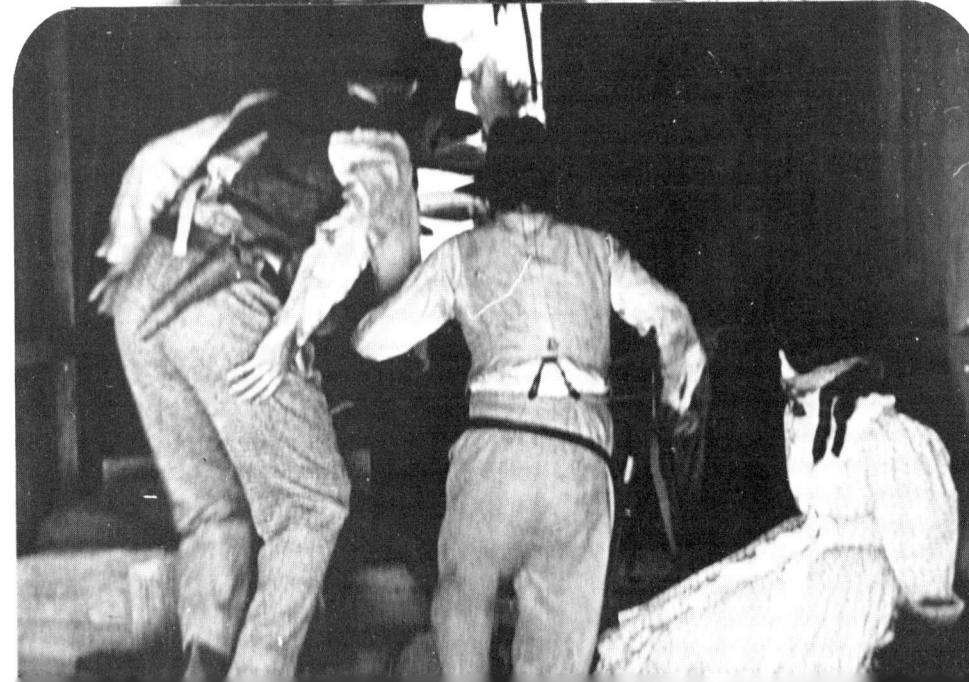

Having successfully thwarted the northern army's plans, Keaton is made a lieutenant in the southern army and is back in the good graces of his sweetheart. But being a lieutenant can post logistical problems for lovers as is illustrated by this final scene from "The General."